AN
Invitation
TO
Theological Study

Charles M. Wood

TRINITY PRESS INTERNATIONAL
Valley Forge, Pennsylvania

Trinity Press International, P.O. Box 851, Valley Forge, PA 19482–0851

Library of Congress Cataloging-in-Publication Data

Wood, Charles Monroe.
    An invitation to theological study / Charles M. Wood.
       p. cm.
    Includes bibliographical references and index.
    ISBN 1-56338-108-7 :
    1. Theology—Study and teaching. 2. Theology. I. Title.
    BV4020.W65 1994
    230'.07—dc20   94-23737
                                              CIP

Printed in the United States of America

95 96 97 98 99   10 9 8 7 6 5 4 3 2 1

Contents

Preface   vii

1. An Invitation to Theological Study   1
   An Address Given at Perkins School of Theology

2. Theological Education and Education
   for Church Leadership   10

3. "Spiritual Formation" and "Theological Education"   24

4. The Knowledge Born of Obedience   35

5. Finding the Life of a Text   45
   Notes on the Explication of Scripture

6. Hermeneutics and the Authority of Scripture   55

7. On Being Known   71

8. On the Reality of God   83

9. The Events in Which God Acts   90

10. The Aim of Christian Theology   98

Notes   109

Index   117

Preface

This volume, which is a collection of essays written over the past several years, has as its common theme the nature and development of theological understanding. The first three chapters deal with that theme directly and comprehensively. Chapter 1, "An Invitation to Theological Study," which originated as an orientation address to the entering class at Perkins School of Theology, sets forth the purpose and uses of a theological education; whereas Chapters 2 and 3, as their titles indicate, relate theological education to education for church leadership and to spiritual formation, respectively.

The next four chapters are concerned more specifically with the task of coming to understand Christian texts and traditions — an indispensable part of theological inquiry, though certainly not the whole of it. Chapter 4, "The Knowledge Born of Obedience," relates understanding and practice. Chapter 5, "Finding the Life of a Text," pursues the same connection with regard to biblical exegesis. Chapter 6, "Hermeneutics and the Authority of Scripture," proposes a way of sorting out questions concerning the theological interpretation of scriptural texts. And Chapter 7, "On Being Known," centers on a practical exercise in the theological interpretation of a biblical passage that is illustrative of the general approach recommended in these chapters.

The focus shifts from texts to concepts for the next two chapters, which deal in turn with the concept of the reality of God and with that of an act of God. It will be clear to the reader throughout, however, that the understanding of Christian texts and the grasp of Christian concepts are vitally linked, and that both are existentially rooted in critical participation in the personal and communal practice of the tradition. The final chapter (the first to be written) returns to the initial subject of the overall aim of theological study and brings together the various motifs of the foregoing chapters.

Although this volume stands on its own, it may also be read as complementing *Vision and Discernment: An Orientation in Theological Study* (Atlanta: Scholars Press, 1985) and *The Formation of Christian Understanding: Theological Hermeneutics* (2d ed., Valley Forge, Pa.: Trinity Press International, 1993).

I am grateful to the publishers of the works in whose pages these chapters first appeared for granting permission for their reappearance in this form. "An Invitation to Theological Study" and "The Aim of Christian Theology" were first published in the *Perkins School of Theology Journal,* volumes 42 and 31, respectively. "Theological Education and Education for Church Leadership" first appeared in *Quarterly Review,* volume 10. " 'Spiritual Formation' and 'Theological Education' " is reprinted from the journal *Religious Education,* volume 86, number 4, by permission from the publisher, The Religious Education Association, 409 Prospect Street, New Haven, CT 06511-2117 (membership information available upon request).

"The Knowledge Born of Obedience" appeared in *Anglican Theological Review,* volume 61, number 3. "Finding the Life of a Text: Notes on the Explication of Scripture" was published in *Scottish Journal of Theology,* volume 31. "Hermeneutics and the Authority of Scripture" was originally published in *Scriptural Authority and Narrative Interpretation,* edited by Garrett Green, copyright © 1987 Fortress Press, and is reprinted by permission of Augsburg Fortress, Minneapolis. "On Being Known" appeared in *Theology Today,* volume 44; "On the Reality of God" was published in *The Iliff Review,* volume 39; and "The Events in Which God Acts" is from *The Heythrop Journal,* volume 22.

An Invitation to Theological Study

An Address Given at Perkins School of Theology

The majority of you gathered here are enrolling in the Master of Divinity program and are aiming for ordination and pastoral ministry. Others, in pursuit of a variety of objectives, are entering the Master of Theological Studies program. There are several entering the Master of Religious Education program, and others are joining the Master of Sacred Music program. Whatever your degree program, nearly all of you understand yourselves to be here pursuing education for some form of ministry. The curricular structure of these various programs is such that you are likely to be having at least some classes together with persons following other degree programs in the school, and you will be sharing — to the extent that your own schedule allows — in the common life of the school of theology. My task is to give you a brief orientation to this enterprise in which we are all about to be involved together, namely, theological education.

Education for ministry — any sort of ministry — involves several things, all interwoven. One thing it involves is what we might call education in Christian life. The authors of a recent book in theology have written: "Coping with God and with [God's] generosity is the central task of Christian faith."[1] Education in Christian life involves learning to trust in God and to be loyal to God — lifelong tasks in themselves, by most accounts. It involves acquiring and refining those habits and practices, emotions and dispositions appropriate to trust in and loyalty to God. It involves coming to understand ourselves in ways appropriate to the Christian message, with its concepts of creation and fall, sin and grace, judgment to the hard of heart and good news to the poor, thanksgiving, joy, patience, and all the rest. All this pertains to education for ministry. In some traditions, this sort of thing has often been discussed under the heading of "spiritual formation" or "spiritual growth"; something like it pertains to all Christian traditions and communities, whether they pay it much explicit attention or not.

Another thing education for ministry involves is education in the Christian faith; that is, growth in understanding the Christian witness — the gospel, the tradition — and what it means when it speaks of God, creation, fall, Jesus Christ, incarnation, atonement, resurrection, and so forth. This is obviously closely related to the type of education just mentioned — education in Christian life, or education as formation — because grasping the central concepts of the Christian faith requires a certain living involvement with them. But the focus here is not so much on the personal appropriation of these concepts or of the Christian message so much as it is on simply grasping the content of the tradition — understanding what the Christian faith is — so that, for instance, you might give an account of it to yourself or to others.

A third thing education for ministry involves is equipment for the particular responsibilities of one's particular vocation in ministry — education in the performance of one's office. That office might be pastoral leadership in a congregation, for which you would presumably need education in the tasks of preaching, counseling, administration, and so forth, and not only in these distinct tasks but in the overall work of pastoral leadership to which they belong. Or perhaps you envision a special ministry in education, or in sacred music, or in community organization, or writing. In any case, there are likely to be particular competences and skills to be acquired, and a certain sense of yourself in the role to be attained, and this too belongs to education for ministry.

It is worth observing that these considerations all apply to education for the general ministry of the church — the ministry that belongs to all Christians — as well as to education for the more specialized ministries of church leadership. All Christians need and deserve competent education in Christian life, education in Christian faith, and education for the particular ways in which they share in the church's task of bearing witness in the world.

Typically, these various processes of education for ministry all start before one arrives in a school of theology — usually long before. There are, of course, many different routes by which people arrive at this place. For some, the route is a process of steady nurture in the life of the church: being raised in the church, actively participating, gradually taking responsibility for leadership in one field or another, perhaps having people point you toward a vocation in special ministry. For many others, the pattern has been different — perhaps early training in the church, leaving, returning later with a new slant on things; or coming to Christianity as an adult, without any real exposure to it before. But however it has happened, you arrive here with some sort of formation as a human being and as a Christian; with some understanding of what the Christian faith is; with some special abilities identified and cultivated. Further, all these educational processes will, we hope, continue long after you leave this place.

A school of theology provides an opportunity for intensive education in all three of these areas — formation, understanding the faith, equipping for ministry. In our setting, formation is given attention through some structured opportunities and occasions — small groups, occasions for corporate worship, workshops, some courses, and the like — but also through our life together. Similarly, understanding the faith is fostered in one way or another through many of the courses you will take and through informal conversation, reading, and reflection. Equipping you for the responsibilities of your ministry is the aim of various other courses and of internships and practica of various kinds (depending on your degree program and your own objectives), and extracurricular opportunities also have a contribution to make.

However, the particular responsibility of a theological school — and your particular responsibility while you are here — is theological education.

What is theological education? The term is not simply a synonym for education for ministry. Nor is theological education something we do alongside other things — something we might do, for instance, in a few specified courses, whereas other courses are devoted to other sorts of education. Rather, theological education is something we do through the whole curriculum and through our life together as a community.

Theological education, simply defined, is that process through which persons become theologians — competent participants in theological inquiry. It is the fostering in persons of an aptitude for theology. Your principal task while you are here is to become theologians — or perhaps I should say, to become better theologians than you are at the moment, whatever your present ability may be. No doubt that is a better way of stating the task, because, just as you have arrived here already with some sort of Christian formation, some understanding of the Christian faith, and some cultivation of your gifts for ministry, so you have arrived with some sort of theological aptitude. It may be relatively good or relatively poor, in need of fine tuning or in need of major overhaul. But in any case, you are already theologians in that you have certain ways of thinking about Christian faith and life and practice, certain ways of forming judgments, certain habits of reflection. Your principal task here is to get much better at all this than you are now.

But why should you? Why should you want to become theologians? What does theology have to do with church leadership? In order to deal with these questions, I need to say something about the nature of Christian theology. Christian theology, as I understand it — and, though I don't claim to speak for my colleagues, I think this is a fairly representative understanding — is a critical inquiry into the validity of Christian witness. That is to say, Christian theology is the activity of examining the life and message of the Christian church, and of making some judgments as to whether they are what they purport to be, namely, authentic, true, and fitting representations of the gospel of Jesus Christ.[2]

One can emphasize the critical aspect of this inquiry — as, for example, when you reflect on some sample of witness already performed (say, the sermon you heard, or perhaps preached, yesterday) — and ask to what extent its witness to the gospel was authentic, intelligible, and appropriate to the occasion. Or one can emphasize the constructive aspect of the inquiry — as, for example, when you ponder next Sunday's worship service or the appeal your church has just received to join in an effort to ban the showing of the film *The Last Temptation of Christ* in your community — and ask what would constitute valid Christian witness in this situation. Both the critical and the constructive aspects are always involved, in every case, though one may be more prominent than the other.

Theological education aims to foster the aptitude for such reflection. I use the word "aptitude" advisedly here; an aptitude is a combination of a capacity and a disposition. To have an aptitude for something is to be apt to do it, under appropriate circumstances; and to be apt to do something you have to be both able to do it and disposed to do it. Ability alone does not make aptitude. Neither does willingness alone. It takes both. In other words, theological education is meant to improve your theological judgment. Its purpose is to make you better at recognizing valid Christian witness should you happen across any; to spot the bad stuff too — the inauthentic, unintelligible, inept stuff that, sad to say, abounds — and furthermore to see what is wrong with it; and to subject not only others' but also (and perhaps foremost) your own past and prospective efforts at witness and at the leadership of witness to searching, constructive criticism.

If at this point you fail to see the connection between theological aptitude and the responsibilities of church leadership, or between theological education and education for ministry, I'm not sure what more I can say. Genuine church leadership is not merely a matter of performing certain prescribed functions or filling certain roles in accord with prevailing expectations; genuine church leadership demands, among other things, imagination, and courage, and something that itself requires both imagination and courage — sound theological judgment. Such judgment is not the exclusive preserve of church leaders, nor is theological education something that concerns them alone. The basic education of all Christians should include a significant theological element: it should equip them for the sort of reflection on the quality of their own Christian faith and life and witness that Christian maturity requires. But it is essential that those entrusted with the special ministries of leadership in the church have an abundant measure of this judgment. It is for this reason that the advanced education for leadership that your various degree programs represent must be theological education.

What does theological education involve? How does one become a theologian? As with learning many things, one becomes a competent participant in theological inquiry by participating in theological inquiry. No one can give you good judgment. You acquire it, if you do, by making judgments, reflecting on your performance in the company of some experienced practitioners who can help you think about what you are doing, and trying again. You acquire it, that is, through participation in a community of theological inquiry. That is what this school tries to be. I appeal to a text that you shortly will be exhorted to read, mark, learn, and inwardly digest — the *Bulletin* of Perkins School of Theology. In its opening paragraph, we are told that "[t]he primary purpose of

Perkins School of Theology is twofold: to serve the church through disciplined reflection on its life and witness, and to prepare women and men for effective leadership in the church." Now, on a superficial reading of this statement, one might conclude that it was talking about two purposes that just happen to be combined here: on the one hand, reflection on the church's life and witness; and on the other, preparation of persons for church leadership. But if the preparation for church leadership that this school offers is essentially theological education, then the unity of purpose is visible. What it boils down to is this: This school prepares women and men for leadership in the church by involving them in disciplined reflection on the church's life and witness — including their own life and witness. It involves them in disciplined reflection on their own Christian existence, on their own understanding of the Christian faith, and on their own practice of ministry. And it does so in such a way as to equip them to engage in such disciplined reflection from then on.

What this involves, more specifically, you shortly will be finding out. For the moment, I should only say — lest there be any doubt on this point — that theological education is a complex affair largely because theological inquiry is a complex affair. Let me mention just two aspects of that complexity. In the first place, theological inquiry involves several distinct academic disciplines, or families of disciplines. In some of your courses, the methodology and approach will be mainly historical; in others, social-scientific concepts and methods — forms of sociology, psychology, and anthropology — will play an important part; in others, various sorts of philosophical inquiry will be prominent. Other courses will combine all of these or will add more besides. To the extent that your previous education has given you some background in these disciplines and has not yet faded irrecoverably from memory, you should be well prepared for what awaits you here. If you come with the advantage of a good liberal education, kept well-tuned, you will find most of what you encounter here to be an extension and enrichment of forms of inquiry you already know. If you do not bring that sort of preparation, or if it needs more than a little dusting off, I hope you will seek out the various sorts of help available to you here in getting oriented to your studies, and that you will then take advantage of the opportunity you have here to get a grounding in the liberal arts by way of your theological education.

The other sort of complexity I want to mention is this. In nearly all of the study you undertake here, you will find yourself expected to engage in a threefold operation that corresponds essentially to the structure of theological inquiry as such. This threefold structure is not unique to theological study, incidentally; it is paralleled in some other fields. But it definitely belongs to theological study. When he described this structure, Martin Luther referred to its elements as *oratio, meditatio,* and *tentatio* — prayer, meditation, and testing — and he claimed to derive this scheme from Psalm 119. "Prayer" here refers to the moment of attentive, receptive listening — openness to being grasped by the subject so that it can make itself known. "Meditation" is the moment of reflection in which questions are posed and judgments are reached. "Testing" refers to the moment of appropriation — that is, of making those judgments your own by incorporating them into your subsequent practice and seeing how they stand up.

For example, suppose that one day in class I declare to you that I am a secular humanist. How might you respond to that declaration? Well, you might just write it down, in true consumer-of-facts style, just in case it should ever come up on an exam ("Is your instructor a secular humanist? — yes or no"), and wait for me to make another noteworthy point. Or you might throw down your pen (or tape recorder) in disgust, exclaiming to your neighbors, "They warned me at home about this school, and they were right!" and resolve to transfer to another school before we do you any more damage.

Or you might undertake a little prayer, meditation, and testing — in Luther's sense of these terms. That is, you might first try to make sure you understand this utterance of mine: What do I mean by the term "secular humanist"? Why would I think it appropriate to describe myself as one? Why am I saying this to the class?

Imagine that by listening attentively, or by asking me questions if you weren't sure you understood, you came to find out that I had uttered this declaration as a way of introducing an argument whose point was to convince you that "secular" and "humanist" should not be regarded as anti-Christian concepts, but rather as concepts with deep roots in the Christian faith. I wanted to suggest to you that true secularity and true humanism were things Christians ought to affirm and stand up for, over against the distorted notions of them current in right-wing religious and political jargon. What I had in mind was genuine biblical secularity, that view of the world as God's good creation which is implied by biblical faith in

God (and which, incidentally, is opposed to all secularisms ancient
or modern), and genuine Christian humanism, that affirmation of
human value which is implied by the gospel's revelation of "the hu-
manity of God" (as Karl Barth put it) in Jesus Christ. You would
perhaps then understand that I was not announcing my conversion
to atheism, as you had at first assumed; you would have grasped
my meaning and my argument, such as it was.

Then you would be in a position to meditate upon this declaration — or, as we might more commonly say, to reflect upon it.
That is, you might ask yourself whether I was right in assigning
those terms the meaning I assigned them and whether my reasons
for associating secularity and humanism with Christian faith, and
for affirming them as good things, and for thus considering myself a secular humanist, were sound reasons. You might, further,
consider whether I showed good judgment in uttering this inflam-
matory declaration to the class. Apart from the merits of my case
for my position, was I more likely to mislead than to inform my
listeners? Under the circumstances, was it wise of me to make that
statement, or was it ill-advised? Having arrived at some judgments
along these lines in your meditation (judgments that might serve
simply to reconfirm your previous views on these points, or that
might open up some new possibilities), you could incorporate those
judgments into your own subsequent reflection and practice, and
test them.

Because our primary goal as your instructors is to nurture in
you this sort of process of inquiry, to exercise and strengthen your
judgment, you will probably notice a disconcerting habit in us: We
keep asking questions, and we keep not giving you the answers. I
don't mean that we will hide our own opinions; ordinarily, we will
share those freely and will explain the reasons behind them as well
as we can. But what we will not do is supply your answers for you.
We continue to insist that you work these out for yourself, and we
are likely to pay more attention to the soundness of the process by
which you arrived at your judgments than to the judgments themselves. You may find this inconvenient. We are prepared for this,
and we will meet your frustration with an equanimity that you will
find most irritating. As your faculty, we have a deep commitment
to your theological education.

In an article in the *American Journal of Theology* in 1916, Professor George Burman Foster of the University of Chicago Divinity
School wrote: "It may be said that usually the candidate for the

ministry — young though he may sometimes be — enters the divinity school as a finished religious and theological product, but that in consequence of his studies there he departs, unfinished, growing, aware that his personality, with its religion and its theology, are alike in the making. A divinity school that achieves such a result has fulfilled its function in the life of the human spirit."[3] As Foster's reference to the age and sex of the typical student makes clear, several things have changed in schools of theology since 1916. But among the things that abide — at least, in schools that take seriously the task of theological education — is this unfinishing effect. Perhaps the uncompleted refurbishing and rearrangement of various classrooms and offices that you have noticed on your arrival this week can serve as an outward sign of an inward truth about our purpose here. As an unfinished and unfinishing school, we welcome you.

2

Theological Education and Education for Church Leadership

The conviction motivating this chapter is that a source of chronic difficulty in the current wide-ranging discussion of the organization and aims of theological study (especially when the discussion touches on the subject of practical theology) is a failure adequately to discriminate among several of the elements involved. When two or more things are not properly distinguished, they cannot be properly related. What usually happens instead is that one somehow absorbs the others, so that their own reality can emerge from time to time only as an anomaly or a disruption. This pattern of absorption and disruption has been played out repeatedly both in theoretical proposals for the reform of theological study and in curricular practice.

My aim here is not to justify this underlying conviction through a critical review of the literature, but rather to undertake a more constructive exploration of some key distinctions that, it seems to me, are essential both to coherent discussion of the issues and to a coherent vision of the structures and aims of theological study. To make these distinctions I have had to sketch out at the relevant points a few elements of a theological, or at least quasi-theological, account of ministry. I hope that these points are phrased with enough generality as to be accessible and useful to people whose full theology of ministry might be quite different from my own.

Writing of the late medieval philosophers with their concern for careful conceptual distinctions and their patience for detail, David Burrell has remarked: "The quest for coherence led to discrimination."[1] Although what is offered here is not exactly an exercise in "philosophical grammar" on the medieval model, it does have the same objective — to help us avoid false generalizations and to see and make appropriate connections.

Key Distinctions

Let us begin with the distinction between *ministry* and *church leadership* — a distinction commonly affirmed in principle and ignored in practice — and, as a sort of corollary, the distinction between education for ministry and education for church leadership.

Church leadership is one sort of ministry, but it is not the whole; education for church leadership is one sort of education for ministry, but it is not the whole. Ministry (that is, service) is the gift and responsibility of all Christians. Indeed, it is the gift and responsibility of all human beings to render service to one another, to other creatures, and thus to God. A properly theological account of ministry would, I think, begin with the ministry of God — that is, with the service God renders — and would place the ministry of creatures (including, but not limited to, that of human beings and of Christians) into that context, as a participation in God's ministry. For the present purpose, we must defer the development of this fuller account and concentrate on a few points regarding the ministry of Christians.

Christians are, without exception, human beings. As such, they are to participate in the service that human creatures are called and enabled to render to fellow-creatures (human and otherwise) and to God. We might call this their human vocation. Christians normally testify that their capacity to understand and fulfill this service has been decisively affected by their own encounter with the Christian tradition, and with God through that tradition (whether primarily by the preached word, the sacraments, the caring of a community, or some other particular means). In one way or another, they have been led to grasp for themselves the story of the universal loss or corruption of the human vocation, of its fulfillment in Jesus Christ, and of the promise of its restoration in themselves and in others — a promise whose realization they may experience, however partially or fitfully, in their own present existence, and for whose completion they hope. Through their participation in Christianity, they are being restored to the human vocation of ministry. Christians need not deny (though some do) that non-Christians may also be given the grace to recover the human vocation, in order to affirm that it is through the Christian faith that they themselves have been given it, and to want to share that possibility with others.

This brings us to the distinctive aspect of the ministry of Christians, namely, their ministry *as* Christians — the service they are called and enabled to render, not simply as human beings, but in their capacity as Christians. We might call this the *Christian* vocation, to distinguish it from the larger human vocation that Christians share with all others. This distinctively Christian ministry is essentially a ministry of witness, or testimony (*marturia*). It is the ministry of enabling others to receive, understand, and appropriate the Christian tradition as a means of grace for their own lives, and to join in turn in its witnessing work. Like ministry in general, this is always to be understood as a participation in the ministry of God. The human enabling of others is itself enabled by God.

This Christian ministry has many parts. It is in some ways corporate and in some ways individual; it is at times "official," that is, explicitly commissioned and sanctioned by the community, and at times unofficial. There are special ministries undertaken by some on behalf of all, and there is the general ministry in which all share simply by participating in the common life of the Christian community. Christian ministry is both explicit and implicit, direct and indirect. For most Christians, it is a ministry carried on along with — and, to a great extent, through — the other activities that occupy us most of the time (making a living, caring for a family, friendships, political action, and so forth), which are at the same time the vehicles through which we exercise our human vocation more or less effectively. For some, the Christian vocation is more nearly and directly a full-time occupation, whether church-commissioned and church-supported or otherwise.

The ministry of church leadership has a similar variety to it. It can be part- or full-time, official or unofficial, "lay" or "professional," individual or corporate. (Actually, each of these distinctions is problematic, particularly when interpreted as a disjunction. They must be handled with care.) Its common task in all its forms is "to equip the saints for the work of ministry, for building up the body of Christ" (Eph. 4:12) — to enable the church to be the church, to guide Christians, individually and corporately, in the exercise of their vocation. At its most basic and comprehensive, this leadership is shared by every Christian in the service one renders to another, grounded in the grace that is given to each "according to the measure of Christ's gift" (Eph. 4:7). In a more particular and limited sense, church leadership is entrusted (in principle, at least) to those whose gifts and opportunities are most appropriate for the specific tasks involved: teaching, nurture, administration, community building, judgment, guidance, and so forth. Although recognizing the common "leadership of all believers" and the great variety of more particular forms of leadership, I will concentrate from this point onward on those kinds of leadership that are ecclesially commissioned, typically full-time, and normally exercised in relation to a congregation or local Christian community.

Education for such leadership is a form of education for ministry and is best understood within that context even though it has some distinctive features. Education for ministry, in turn, is one aspect of the broader enterprise of Christian education, understood as that whole complex of educational activities by means of which persons are received into the Christian community and are prepared — not just initially, but continually — for responsible participation in that community. Not only the more focused and deliberate occasions of teaching and learning in the church — church-school classes, study groups, and so on — but also the educational aspect of the community's ritual and sacramental life, of its care for its members in crises, and of all of its other activities, belongs to Christian education thus comprehensively understood.

Within that enterprise, three distinct (though certainly closely related) components may be identified. There is, first, that educational activity through which we attain our knowledge of the Christian tradition and of our own particular ecclesial tradition — the doctrines, events, institutions, persons, and so forth, that make the tradition what it is. From this we gather our own sense of what the Christian faith is all about. We could call this "education in Christian faith." Second, there is what might be called "education in Christian life." This is the lifelong process of coming to understand ourselves and our world in ways appropriate to the Christian message, with its key life-shaping concepts — ways of learning to trust in God and to be loyal to God; to acquire the attitudes, dispositions, perceptions, and so forth that are appropriate to such trust and loyalty, and thus to take on a certain kind of human and Christian identity. The third component we can designate "education for ministry," so long as we recognize that each of the other two is in its own way also education for ministry. The specific contribution of this third aspect is to equip us with the particular competencies we need in order to play our part in the Christian community's ongoing life of witness and service.

These three components are closely interdependent, and the order in which they have just been mentioned should not be taken to imply some inherent logical or pedagogical ordering of them. Understanding the Christian faith requires training in Christian life, and vice versa; and neither is possible apart from some initiation into the practice of Christian witness, both corporate and individual.[2] Nor is the third a possibility without the other two. Receiving the Christian witness and being formed by it; understanding that witness and one's own place in it, so as to affirm it for oneself; and coming to *bear* witness, to share the community's distinctive ministry, are all three ongoing, interwoven elements of Christian existence.

Although the three are inseparable, it is within the third, education for ministry, that we may more specifically locate education for church leadership. As we will see, education for church leadership requires a particular intensification of all three aspects of Christian education. This is because church leadership itself demands certain sorts of spiritual maturity and certain ways of understanding the Christian faith, as well as certain capacities for the exercise of leadership, that are not required of all Christians. But because all of these special requirements are ordered to preparation for the ministry of leadership, it is in relation to that aim that they are best understood.

Of course, church leadership is one of many sorts of ministry for which some particular educational preparation is required. Acknowledging that ministry and church leadership are not synonymous terms, and then referring exclusively to education for church leadership as education for ministry or ministerial education, is one way of negating in practice what one affirms in principle. Anyone who undertakes a course of study so as to be better equipped to serve God and fellow-creature is engaged in education for ministry — and a relatively small proportion of that education goes on in schools of theology.

Some Dangers in Labels

Education for church leadership is frequently referred to as "theological education" — an equation that carries dangers as well as values. Although the two enterprises are associated, they should not be merely equated. The distinction and relation between theological education and education for church leadership deserves some careful exploration.

Theological education, in the most strict and proper sense, is the process through which persons acquire an aptitude for theology. An aptitude for Christian theology is a capacity and disposition to engage in critical reflection upon the Christian witness (which means, upon what is conveyed by everything that Christians are, say, and do as Christians, singly and together), aimed at testing the adequacy of that witness in terms of its own claims to validity.[3] The three ingredients of the claim to validity that any act of Christian witness at least implicitly makes, as I understand it, are (1) the claim to be authentically Christian, that is, to represent faithfully the gospel of Jesus Christ; (2) the claim to be meaningful and true; and (3) the claim to be fitting, or appropriate to the context.[4] Theological reflection can take the form of a critical examination of some actual sample of Christian witness — something said or done by Christians in their capacity as Christians — to see to what extent this act of witness lives up to its own intentions to be authentic, true, and fitting to the situation. Or it can take the more constructive (though no less critical) form of asking what valid witness would amount to under a given set of circumstances.

Some aptitude for Christian theology is requisite to Christian life itself. This does not mean that every Christian must be a theological scholar, nor even that she or he must be cognizant of what theological scholars are up to. It only means that every Christian, under normal circumstances, inevitably is called to make judgments as to what constitutes valid Christian witness, accepting or rejecting certain alternatives. Such judgments are involved from fairly early on in each person's Christian education, as well as in the ordinary course of Christian existence. It is for this reason that one element of Christian education, touching on all three principal components of that enterprise, is theological education. In the course of making those judgments as to the nature of Christian faith, life, and practice that are involved in coming to be a Christian, people learn, from those who teach them in these matters, how to make judgments. Depending on how they are taught, they learn to judge well or poorly, reluctantly or willingly, haphazardly or with deliberation. They acquire some sort of theological aptitude, which plays an important role in determining the sort of Christian identity they take on, the way they understand the faith, and the quality of the witness they bear. A Christian community has no choice as to whether theological education, for all its members, will be an element of its educational work; it only has a choice as to the kind of theological education it will be.

The role of theological education in education for church leadership is especially crucial, because it has a large part in determining the quality of judgment of those responsible for the nurture and guidance of the rest of the community. The greater the scope of leadership, the more serious this becomes. It is altogether appropriate, then, that those institutions responsible for the most rigorous and intensive preparation of church leaders be known as theological schools. It is far more important, however, that these institutions actually *be* theological schools and that the education they provide aspiring church leaders be, from start to finish, genuine theological education.

Three Components of Christian Education

The theological education of church leaders, like that of other Christians, must give attention to all three of those components of Christian education outlined earlier: education in Christian faith, education in Christian life, and education for Christian ministry.

I said earlier that education for church leadership requires a particular intensification and development of these three components. The way in which this is so must not be misunderstood. So far as education in Christian life is concerned, we should not think that church leadership demands a higher Christian proficiency than other forms of ministry. It is a mistake to assume that anyone who shows signs of seriousness and promise in the Christian life should automatically be steered toward preparation for church leadership, for there are other kinds of ministry at least as demanding of spiritual maturity and all that it involves. There are, however, certain aspects of spiritual maturity, certain dispositions and traits of character, that are particularly (though not exclusively) pertinent to certain forms of church leadership.

For example, pastors and those in similar positions of leadership need to know themselves well. Leadership in general is full of temptations. Further, the professional roles occupied by such church leaders in our society give ample opportunity for various kinds of abuse. Self-deception, as well as the deception of others, is an easy and attractive feature of religious leadership. Misuse of time and resources, manipulation of others by means of one's professional knowledge and power, and other forms of malfeasance are not only possible, but are often subtly encouraged by the social arrangements in which church leaders find themselves and the psychological dynamics of the situation. Persons preparing for such work must know their own hearts in this regard; they must be well acquainted with their own strengths and weaknesses when faced by such challenges, and with the opportunities that both the strengths and the weaknesses afford for genuine and effective service.[5]

Church leaders are also typically called upon to know the hearts of others. If they are to provide leadership to congregations and individuals under all sorts of conditions, they must understand human behavior in health and adversity. This requires some degree of psychological, anthropological, and sociological understanding, as well as a theological grasp of the human condition before God. It also requires insight and penetration, receptivity and generosity, and a multitude of other personal qualities that rest finally upon one's self-knowledge and on the character of one's spiritual life. In these and other ways, the responsibilities of church leadership call for some special attention to the quality of the Christian existence of those being prepared for it.

Similar points can be made concerning the particular needs of church leaders in the other two component areas of Christian education. So far as their education in the Christian faith is concerned, to the extent that church leaders are responsible for guiding the church in its preservation and extension of the Christian tradition, their education must involve their acquiring not only a more extensive factual knowledge of that tradition than that ordinarily expected of other Christians, but also an understanding of how the tradition works and a sure ability to distinguish authentic tradition — that which mediates the genuine gospel — from its counterfeits. It is not necessary that they have the erudition of professional historians of Christianity, but it is necessary that they have an ability to work with the tradition as it bears upon their responsibilities of leadership (for example, teaching the faith to others, answering questions about what Christian belief involves, sharing in the task of formulating and explicating the community's doctrines, or equipping people to discern what is going on when they are confronted with competing claims about the faith).

With regard to education in the task of leadership, it is clear that pastoral leadership, for example, requires a number of identifiable abilities in such areas as administration, counseling, preaching, group leadership, and teaching. Basic competence in the functions pertaining to one's own role and its expectations is essential: one must know how to conduct a meeting, deliver a sermon, plan a service of worship, and so forth, and part of one's education for leadership is acquiring and continuing to strengthen those specific capabilities. But there is an aspect of the competence of leadership whose presence or absence in a person, though not so visible as the quality of her or his skill in a particular area of functioning, is ultimately far more important. This is the capacity for critical reflection on what one is doing as a leader, through each and all of the activities and roles that one's leadership involves — the capacity to transcend the obvious demands and expectations of one's office and to think about the direction and effect of what one is doing in relation to the mission of the church in the situation. An aptitude for that sort of reflection will not compensate for the lack of basic skills in the practice of one's ministry. It is not, by itself, sufficient qualification for church leadership. But no amount of technical virtuosity as preacher, counselor, and so on, will make up for the absence or immaturity of that judgment on which genuine leadership, as distinguished from the competent fulfillment of certain role expectations, depends.

This brief account of the ways in which education for church leadership must address each of the three component areas of Christian education may begin to make clearer why it must involve theological education at every point. Essentially, what this account indicates is that church leadership requires a well-developed aptitude for theological self-criticism, for theological understanding of the Christian faith, and for theological criticism of one's performance in leadership. The theological education of church leaders, then, must address all three of these. It can do so adequately only if all three are explicitly brought under scrutiny in some way in the course of one's theological study.

It must be kept in mind that the aim of *theological* education as such is not to form Christians, but to form the habit of critical reflection on one's formation. It is not to mediate the content of the Christian tradition, but to equip one for theological reflection on the Christian tradition. It is not to train in leadership skills, but to cultivate an aptitude for reflection on the quality of one's own and others' leadership as an instrument of the church's witness. The service of theology to witness, and hence of theological education to Christian education, is best conceived as an indirect one: it is the service performed by reflection upon a practice, rather than by the practice itself. This is a genuine and even an indispensable service. But whenever the distinction between theology and witness or between theological education and Christian education is forgotten or denied — as it frequently seems to be — that unique service is lost.[6]

Distinct as these educational processes are, in the education of church leaders they cannot be separated. Learning to reflect theologically on one's formation not only presupposes that formation is going on, but is a part of one's formation. Learning to reflect theologically on leadership must be ingredient in the process of acquiring the specific abilities for leadership, or it is not likely to become second nature to the leader, as it should. And the process of understanding and appropriating the Christian tradition already involves the making of theological judgments and the gaining of some sort of competence in that enterprise. Theological education of the sort that theological schools conduct is not a separate stage of education to be entered upon only after one has already acquired the other requisites for church leadership. One might think of the theological school as the medium or the context within which one's development in these three areas is given some important nourishment and brought to a new level of maturity precisely through theological study. Certainly, one's Christian education (including one's education for ministry) normally begins long before one enters a school of theology and continues long after one leaves. The distinctive contribution of the school of theology to education for church leadership is to strengthen the theological aspect of that education, across its entire range.

Differences Among Theological Schools

In carrying out their responsibility for the theological education of church leaders, theological schools differ considerably among themselves with regard both to their explicit intentions and to their actual accomplishments. Some of the differences are matters of principle: for instance, commitment to a particular ecclesiology or a particular understanding of ministry will lead a school to a certain set of objectives and decisions that will set it apart from schools grasped by different commitments. Other differences are the results of historical or social factors. A school will do well to reflect from time to time upon both its explicit aims and those other factors in its situation that are shaping its work.

As a stimulus to such reflection, let me risk some impressionistic generalizations about one group of schools that, despite various differences of academic and ecclesiastical affiliation, share a common legacy — those institutions founded and largely maintained by what until recently we have called the mainline Protestant denominations in the United States. These schools generally seem to do a better job of teaching students to reflect on the Christian tradition than of teaching them to reflect on their own Christian existence or to reflect on the quality of their leadership. This is not to say that the schools spend more time on education in Christian faith than they do on education in Christian life or on education for ministry; the proportion of time given to each varies a great deal from place to place or tradition to tradition. It is rather to say that the schools are better at teaching students to deal *theologically* with the content of the tradition than with either their own lives or their vocation as church leaders. Such education as goes on in these latter two areas is relatively less theological in character, as a rule. With regard to Christian spirituality or formation, it is more likely to consist in a straightforward extension of basic Christian education (often of a remedial sort); and in the area of education for ministry, it is more likely to concentrate on conveying a basic functional competence in the role. My impression is that the calls which such schools frequently hear that they should give more attention to spiritual formation or to the cultivation of students' professional competence for ministry are rarely cries for more *theological* attention to these areas, but rather for more basic "first-order" education in Christian life and in meeting the needs of congregations.

At the same time, in the area in which these schools do relatively well at theological (as distinguished from Christian) education, they generally do a better job at teaching students to pursue the questions of the authenticity and of the meaningfulness and truth of Christian witness than to pursue the question of its fittingness to its context. Courses in Bible and history may encourage students to think about the origins and transmission of the Christian tradition, its continuity and its transformation through time, and raise (at least implicitly) the theological question of the authenticity of contemporary witness. Courses in systematic theology tend to pursue this question, sometimes in conjunction with the more philosophically oriented question of meaning and truth. Indeed, the task of systematic theology is often formulated as that of mediating the demands of authenticity or faithfulness to what has been received, and of meaningfulness or credibility in the contemporary world. Courses in what is sometimes called "practical theology" (the fourth division of the conventional fourfold curriculum, in addition to biblical, historical, and systematic studies) are for the most part courses aimed at teaching the various more or less discrete competences required of pastors and other church leaders, and their teachers tend to identify themselves with the specific disciplines concerned (homiletics, pastoral care, education, and so on) rather than with practical theology as such.

Accounting for the emergence and maintenance of such a state of affairs in modern theological education is a task for social historians. Rather than attempt any such interpretation, I want to concentrate on a conceptual problem that, although it is not solely responsible for the tendencies just identified, seems to me to have done a great deal to encourage them. The problem has to do with the use of the term "practical theology" to designate two distinct sorts of inquiry and instruction, each legitimate and necessary in its own right. The failure to distinguish properly between them has sometimes led to a sort of competition between them for the title, which has not served the real interests of either. I would not want to claim that the multitude of uses of the term "practical theology" can finally be reduced to these two. My claim is rather that if these two were appropriately distinguished and recognized as legitimate and complementary enterprises rather than as rival understandings of one task, it would do something to reduce the current confusion that tends to weaken both.

One contender is that dimension of theological study whose particular responsibility is to pursue the question as to the fittingness of Christian witness to its context. The other contender is that sort of theological study whose subject matter is church leadership — typically, pastoral leadership. The first is distinguished by the particular aspect of the validity question that it pursues; the second, by the particular subject matter it investigates.

One reason it has proven difficult to keep these two distinct is that each of them involves the other. Theological reflection on the fittingness of Christian witness to its context includes (but is not limited to) reflection on the role of church leadership — of the institutions, activities, and so forth, through which leadership is exercised — in enabling (or preventing) that witness to be fitting to its context. Theological reflection on church leadership — that is, on the ways in which the structures, activities, and so forth, of leadership work to further or hinder valid Christian witness — includes (but is not limited to) reflection on the fittingness of that leadership to its context. If, as sometimes happens, the church is identified with its leadership, and Christian witness reduced to the activity of church leaders, the distinction between these two intersecting inquiries becomes that much more difficult to see.

In my own constructive account of the organization of theological study, I have reserved the name of practical theology for the first of these contending enterprises.[7] It is one of the three primary theological disciplines, each of which corresponds to one of the three constitutive dimensions of Christian theology. (In this account, the question of the Christian authenticity of the witness belongs to historical theology, and the question of its meaningfulness and truth to philosophical theology.)

When it has not been called practical theology, a name that has sometimes been assigned to the second of these enterprises is pastoral theology. Pastoral theology has often been conceived and taught in such a way as to combine theological reflection on church leadership (specifically, on the office and duties of the pastor) with theological reflection on the personhood of the leader (that is, on the pastor's own life and Christian self-understanding, particularly in relation to the responsibilities of leadership). Thus, it deals from a theological standpoint with both the "education in Christian life" and the "education for ministry" of the candidate for church leadership, and has gone some way toward addressing the lack of attention to these two areas in the typical theological curriculum. There is much to be said for this approach, so long as it is not seen as an *alternative* to practical theology (as I have used the term above), but rather as a sort of concentration of theological attention upon the theme of church leadership and upon the education of the leader. Both practical theology and pastoral theology (if we are to use these names for them) have a place in education for church leadership — the former as a necessary component of theological education as such, and the latter as a means of acquiring the aptitude for theological self-examination that is necessary to genuine leadership.

There are some difficulties, however, with the name of "pastoral theology" for the second of these pursuits. In conventional Protestant usage, pastoral theology is concerned with "the pastoral office and its function" — that is, with the role and activity of the pastor in the congregation. Unless all church leadership is somehow to be assimilated to the pastoral office, the term has some obvious limitations as a designation for the theological examination of church leadership. Its use may also give some privileged weight to the concept or image of "shepherd" as a key to the understanding of church leadership — a privilege that may or may not be theologically warranted.[8] At the same time, in Roman Catholic usage — and increasingly in Protestant usage as well — "pastoral theology" has come to refer not to that discipline which deals with the office and function of the pastor, but rather to that which deals with the pastoral activity of the church as a whole, as well as with the pastoral activity of its leaders. It concerns itself with the care that the church provides to people, and its scope may be considerably broader than was previously thought — extending to the church's care for nonmembers as well as members, and to a care that is exercised through social and political action as well as on the individual level.

It is not clear, then, that "pastoral theology" is the best term to use for the theological examination of church leadership. Perhaps a better term, enabling a better grasp of what this study involves, will emerge. What is crucial, in my judgment, is that the two inquiries I have here described be clearly distinguished and that both of them be affirmed as properly belonging to theological education for church leadership.

3

"Spiritual Formation" and "Theological Education"

Concern for and perplexity about the place of spiritual formation in theological education have become generally visible among theological students, faculty and administration, and within the churches in the last two decades, and they continue unabated. There are several reasons for this. The cultural transformation of North America since World War II is undoubtedly the main factor putting this issue on the agenda of theological schools. Today, neither the typical seminarian nor the congregation (if any) from which she or he comes shows the kind of socialization into and internalization of the religious tradition that was characteristic of seminarians and churches as recently as the 1940s, and the schools have not yet taken stock of what this means for their work nor learned how to cope with it.[1]

Another factor, related to this one in some complex ways, is the rise of new kinds of difference in many theological schools. The new visibility of traditions previously suppressed or ignored (for example, African-American and Hispanic traditions), the resurgence of evangelicalism within "main-line" Protestant denominations, a new diversity within some evangelical communities themselves, and the growing impact of feminist thought and practice have all led to a situation in which the contested character of "the Christian tradition" is inescapably evident. What is it, finally, to be a Christian? Into just which tradition or community should we expect students to be socialized?

A school that tries to address this change in the situation of its students by deliberately playing a greater role in their spiritual formation than it was accustomed to play in the past may encounter a number of problems. For example, the increasing and increasingly evident diversity of background and conviction within both the student body and the faculty of many theological schools is often perceived as a complicating factor when it comes to spiritual formation. (There are certainly other ways of regarding diversity than as an inconvenience; but this is how it is often perceived in this connection, especially by those who can recall what seemed to be a simpler time.) An approach to spiritual formation that presupposes homogeneity of background, tradition, or commitment is likely to run into difficulty on that score alone.

There is also the question of the compatibility between the enterprise of forming persons in a faith and the enterprise of teaching them to reflect critically upon that faith. Does the task of spiritual formation have any legitimate place in a theological school? Those who work or study in schools with a strong "seminary" identity, where formation is seen as the principal task, might regard this as an odd question. In any event, they would have far less difficulty giving an affirmative answer to it than would many in schools where the primary pedagogical mission is seen as that of equipping students to engage in theological reflection in its various aspects. In neither case, however, is the answer as simple as it may have seemed twenty or more years ago, given the transformations those years have wrought both within the schools and in the culture of which they are a part. Further, among those who grant that spiritual formation may have a legitimate place in theological education, few are inclined to think that there is anything at all simple about the answer to the next question: What sort of place does it have? What is its role?

What does "spiritual formation" have to do with "theological education"? What does "theological education" have to do with "spiritual formation"? I have put these two terms in quotation marks simply as a reminder that each of them may be used in several different senses. How one conceives of the relationship between spiritual formation and theological education will depend in large part upon the sense in which one is taking each term. When participants in discussions on this subject have different senses of the key terms in mind, it is easy for them to talk past each other. My aim here is show how some sorting out and clarification of the senses in which these terms are employed might lead to more illuminating and productive discussions.

I do not propose to catalogue all the conceivable uses of these two terms, but rather to identify one fairly generic, avowedly non-theological understanding of "spiritual formation" and relate it to three distinct senses of "theological education." Of course, no understanding of spiritual formation is innocent of theological implications. Even the term itself is not. It is important, then, to keep in mind that this one may set up the discussion so as to favor certain possibilities or emphasize certain issues while overlooking others. The generic understanding I will employ is one recently set out by George Lindbeck.

Lindbeck characterizes spiritual formation as "the deep and personally committed appropriation of a comprehensive and coherent outlook on life and the world." Such formation, as Lindbeck describes it, is not simply a matter of external behavior; those who are "well-formed" in a given outlook "have to a significant degree developed the capacities and dispositions to think, feel, and act in accordance with their world view no matter what the circumstances."[2]

Spiritual formation, for Lindbeck, is to be distinguished from conversion and commitment, and also from psychological and moral formation, because all of these are, at least in some respects, independent variables. In affirming these distinctions, Lindbeck implicitly raises some very important issues. For example: Just what is the relation between spiritual formation and a commitment of faith? Could one, in principle, be "well-formed" in a tradition, that is, develop the capacities and dispositions that are normally associated with competent participation in it, without being an adherent of that tradition? Or again: Granted that psychological, moral, and spiritual maturity are not identical, just how are they related? Are these three distinct *aspects* of human character, or are they three distinct *ways of describing* human character — or a mixture of both? As we will see, these issues emerge with some practical force in the context of theological education.

Lindbeck's is a generic description of spiritual formation in that it is meant to depict something that occurs not only in those strands of the Christian tradition in which the term and concept "spiritual formation" developed, but also in other strands of Christian tradition, other religious traditions, and even such non-religious (or quasi-religious) traditions and outlooks as some forms of humanism and Marxism. What is crucial to the description is the notion of the development of those capacities and dispositions that are appropriate to the outlook or worldview in question, whatever it may be. The description is nontheological in that it does not involve or imply reference to God, or to anything roughly analogous to God. It is nonnormative in that it says nothing about the sorts of capacities and definitions that people *should* develop; material judgments as to what it is to be "well-formed" or "spiritually mature" are judgments internal to a tradition, and this description leaves them so.

A final interesting feature of Lindbeck's definition — another point on which it is neutral, so to speak — is that it implies no judgment as to how the *process* of spiritual formation is to be conceived. In those branches of Christian tradition where the term itself is most at home, "formation" is viewed as a deliberate undertaking in which those who are spiritually more mature direct and assist the less mature, and "forming" is seen as an apt term for this process: there are various disciplines and exercises aimed at shaping the Christian life, helping one acquire the proper habits (or virtues) and shed inappropriate ones, and so forth. But in other Christian communities, the very idea of "forming" is suspect, as running counter to the way human personhood ought to be described as well as to the way the Holy Spirit works with and in human beings: "Where the Spirit of the Lord is, there is freedom (2 Cor. 3:17) and therefore not 'formation,'" as one writer summarizes this position.[3] Sanctification is God's work — not the product of human programs; further, "forming" is not as accurate a term for what the Spirit does as, say, "regeneration." Most of those who take this alternative to the language of "formation" still find appropriate ways of nurturing and guiding persons in the life of faith, and ways of describing the spiritual state of the unregenerate and the regenerate, the immature and the mature Christian — but with some characteristic differences in both conception and procedure. There are similar ranges of variation among Christian groups as to, for example, the role involvement in Christian practice plays in spiritual formation — and as to what sort of Christian practice is most crucial. (Availing oneself of the instituted means of grace? Participating in the praxis of liberation?)

Admittedly, Lindbeck's is a very formal and spare description of spiritual formation, with limited usefulness. It cannot take the place of accounts that are normative, theological, and tradition-specific, and that take positions in accord with those commitments on the various issues involved — and it is not intended to do so.

For the purposes of this sort of discussion, however, it may prove helpful.

Spiritual Formation in Education for Church Leadership

"Theological education" is frequently used as a term to designate formal education for the special ministries of the church, particularly for ministries of church leadership such as the priesthood or pastorate.[4] What is the role of spiritual formation in education for church leadership? That a religious leader should be well-formed in the capacities and dispositions belonging to the tradition seems obvious, but it may be worthwhile to examine the obvious. Why is spiritual maturity a requisite for leadership? What sort of spiritual maturity is requisite? One might identify a number of relatively distinct needs in this connection. To the extent that the leader is expected to serve as spiritual guide or spiritual director for others (and the extent varies from one tradition or community to another), there will be particular demands upon her or his own spirituality. As teachers of the tradition, leaders are generally expected to know whereof they speak, and this demands some sort of internalization of the tradition and competence in living out of its resources. Dealing with the pressures and temptations of the leadership role itself may require a certain spiritual (as well as moral and psychological) insight and strength. All these expectations, and others, might be seen to call for particular sorts of spiritual aptitude.

It might be argued, however, that however one weighs these various expectations and their implications for the spiritual preparation of the candidate for church leadership, most crucial to the overall function of leadership is the leader's capacity to think with and on behalf of the tradition — a capacity that depends partly upon the leader's having acquired or appropriated the tradition in a deepgoing way, and partly upon the leader's being able to maintain a sort of critical distance from the tradition at the same time. On this view, a person who is simply indoctrinated into the tradition and who appropriates it zealously and uncritically is probably a poor candidate for a position of genuine leadership. If placed in a leadership role, such a person is often susceptible to manipulation by others — or, lacking that susceptibility, can be even more dangerous because of the lack of critical checks on her or his own perceptions and convictions. At the same time, a leader who is not well-formed in the tradition is likely to be inept and ineffective no matter what abilities for critical reflection she or he may possess. What is needed is a combination of thorough internalization and critical perspective. Michael Walzer's depiction of the position of the "ideal social critic" would seem to pertain to church leadership as well: "A little to the side, but not outside: critical distance is measured in inches."[5] Can we look upon the acquisition of a capacity for self-transcendence as something that belongs to the spiritual formation of church leaders? This is not to say that it does not belong to the formation of every Christian; only that it may be particularly important for those who assume leadership in the community.

To what extent can spiritual formation for church leadership be a deliberate undertaking? To what extent can and should it be distinct from the formation of Christians generally? Where does it belong — that is, in what context, at what points in one's preparation for leadership, is it best conducted? Whose responsibility is it? These are some of the questions that arise in this connection. Some clarity on them may be attained by considering the matter in relation to the other two senses of "theological education."

Theological Education and Spiritual Formation

A second sense of the term "theological education" — and, as I see it, its most proper sense — is "education in theology": theological education is that process through which persons become theologians, that is, competent participants in theological inquiry. If an aptitude for theology is one requirement for church leadership, then theological education in this sense of the term is one component of education for church leadership. It is not the whole: leadership requires more than theological aptitude. But it is an indispensable component, in most understandings of what genuine church leadership involves. In fact, one could say that the process through which one acquires that capacity for self-transcendence with respect to one's own appropriation of the tradition that was mentioned above is nothing other than theological education. In this regard, theological education is one aspect of the spiritual formation of church leaders — and, indeed, of Christians generally. To the extent that every Christian needs to be able to reflect on his or her own faith and practice and upon that of the community in order to exercise his or her own vocation as a Christian, theological education is a necessary component of every Christian's education. To the extent that church leadership requires a particular measure of competence in such reflection, theological education of a more advanced and specialized sort is a necessary component of education for church leadership.

Can this rightly be regarded as an aspect of *spiritual* formation? If spiritual formation is to be distinguished from psychological and moral formation, how does the attainment of an aptitude for theological inquiry belong to one's spiritual formation? An adequate response to this question would require a fuller and more specific account both of the nature of theology and of what spiritual formation involves than it is appropriate to offer here, but some of the ingredients of a response can be suggested. First, because theology is a form of reflection on the Christian tradition, it requires a knowledge of that tradition. (For "tradition" here, one might substitute "faith" or "witness" or any of various other terms representing what David Kelsey calls "the Christian thing.") Part of that knowledge is the sort of conceptual competence that goes with being "well-formed" in the tradition. That is, one must know how the key concepts of the tradition — God, grace, sin, creation, hope, and so forth — actually work in the practice of the community. Theological education, then, involves a deliberate broadening and deepening of one's own experience of the Christian "thing" as a necessary base for one's reflection.

What frequently happens in theological education, however, is something quite different from this. Rather than having their existential grasp of the tradition broadened and deepened, theological students often perceive that their instructors are out to deprive them of their piety. They respond either by allowing that to happen and drifting into some sort of cynicism, or by constructing a protective shell around their faith so as to prevent theological education from penetrating to their own convictions and practices. In either case, the result is a failure of theological education: it does not have the material it needs on which to work. From a practical, pedagogical standpoint alone, theological instruction must include constructive "formative" experience that opens up the tradition to students (and vice versa) in ways they have not, for the most part, previously attained. This requires certain gifts on the part of faculty, and certain insights about teaching and learning, and a certain environment if it is to happen, and happen in such a way as to enhance rather than hinder the overall process.

This sort of experience with Christianity, the acquisition of the conceptual competence it takes to "see things Christianly" and to understand the tradition from the inside, is possible, I think, for the non-Christian as well as for the committed Christian. This is a contested point, of course, and because the vast majority of those involved in Christian theological education understand themselves to be Christians, it may seem to raise an unnecessary issue here. But both those who affirm and those who deny the possibility should consider the implications of their position for the relation of spiritual formation to theological education. For example, if one is to say that only a Christian can understand the Christian tradition (and thus that only a Christian can engage in Christian theological study), one must be able to specify in what "being a Christian" consists and how this qualifies one to understand. One must further be able to show why someone who is not a Christian, by this definition, is thereby disqualified from understanding. Because what it is to be a Christian is a matter of some dispute within the Christian tradition, any such specification is likely to meet with controversy. It might be more productive to begin with this question: What sort of personal involvement with the Christian tradition is necessary to attain the understanding of it that theological instruction presupposes? Among other things, this question will prompt some grappling with the issue of what is meant by "the Christian tradition" in its unity and diversity — and with the related problems and opportunities that this diversity presents for spiritual formation.

Some amount of spiritual formation (that is, of the acquisition of those personal conceptual capacities that enable one to understand the tradition), then, is requisite to theological education. There is also a sense in which theological education is requisite to spiritual formation. An aptitude for critical reflection on "the Christian thing," including one's own convictions about it, pertains to Christian spiritual maturity. To be willing and able to trust in God more than in one's own beliefs about God; to hold oneself open to the possibility of correction with regard to one's most cherished convictions and practices; in short, to see theology as a means to ongoing repentance and renewal is to have grasped something of its spiritual significance. And the process of acquiring theological aptitude is, accordingly, one factor in the process of growth toward spiritual maturity. Correspondingly, one is unlikely to develop and sustain an aptitude for theological reflection if one has not developed the spiritual resources that make it possible to live with and even welcome the challenges it brings.

It appears, then, that theological education in this second, stricter sense has a role in spiritual formation, and that at least some elements of spiritual formation — elements having to do with the capacities for understanding and criticism that belong to the theological task — have a role in theological education.

Spiritual Formation and the Theological School

A third sense in which the term "theological education" is often employed is as a way of referring collectively to those institutions devoted to formal theological education, in either or both of the senses previously considered. In the North American context, the term is applied in this way especially to those graduate professional schools in which persons receive their specific academic preparation for specialized ministries. What does spiritual formation have to do with the enterprise of theological education, thus understood? What is the place of spiritual formation in the work of the theological school?

Theological schools differ in all sorts of significant ways, and some of these ways have implications for the answer one gives to this question. Some schools stress theological education in the second sense we have considered: their mission, as they see it, is to develop students' aptitudes for theological inquiry, whatever the students' vocational aims may be. Other schools stress theological education in the first sense considered: their mission is to prepare leaders for the church. Depending on what they take such preparation to involve, theological education in the second sense will have a larger or smaller role in their programs, and it will be coordinated with other sorts of education that pertains to qualification for church leadership. Some such schools focus their efforts on spiritual formation, and everything else is ordered somehow to that mission. Others are less comfortable with the image of "seminary" than with that of professional school; there the focus is on professional education for the specialized tasks of church leadership. Some schools regard themselves as part of the church (and, often, as an integral part or agency of the specific church bodies that own or fund them) and conduct spiritual formation for their students on behalf of the church, as a part of the students' ongoing Christian education. Other schools are independent of church sponsorship or control and are more reluctant to engage in what they perceive as a churchly task, either in view of the diversity of their constituencies or because they think it inappropriate for an academic institution to engage in such a function. Some schools combine various of these features — and are pulled in various directions.[6]

To stipulate what role spiritual formation should play in "the theological school" would require an understanding of what constitutes a theological school and of what belongs to its mission, regardless of the specific variables just mentioned. My own inclination would be to say that what is constitutive of a theological school is its pursuit of theological education in what I take to be the proper sense of the term, that is, in the second sense mentioned above. (A theological school, then, need not have education for church leadership as its aim — odd as that may sound, given our conventional notion of what a theological school is! Furthermore, a school whose aim is education for church leadership may fail to be a theological school if it allows other aspects of education for leadership to compromise or crowd out its training in theological inquiry. In this case, though, I would wonder with what validity it might claim to be providing education for church leadership.) This would mean that spiritual formation would be involved in the work of the school in the two basic ways sketched under that heading: insofar as theological reflection and training in it *presuppose* spiritual formation, and insofar as they *constitute* spiritual formation, formation is something to which the theological school must give deliberate attention.

How much the school can accomplish in this area is another question. Granted that a certain spiritual maturity is requisite to theological education, how much of this can the school itself foster, and in what ways? What part of this belongs to the curriculum and to the teaching-learning relationship? How much to other aspects of the school's life? Are there ways in which the school might more properly *provide for* the formation of its students — in collaboration with churches or other agencies, perhaps — rather than taking a more direct hand in it? What initiative on the part of the school is appropriate, and how much must be either left to the students themselves or assumed by other bodies (congregations, student communities, and so on)?

A theological school that, like most of those we know, has the more comprehensive objective of preparing persons for church leadership — whether the focus in this regard is on formation, on professional education, or elsewhere — will both want and need to do still more with spiritual formation than this. Just how much more and how it will be achieved depend on its specific objectives and situation. How to achieve these additional objectives without endangering its primary identity and mission as a theological school is a question always to be borne in mind. My own conviction, however, is that the more a theological school keeps its primary identity as a place for the teaching and learning of theology clearly in mind, the better its chances of realizing these other objectives in ways that foster the development of genuine leadership for the church. And a related conviction is that the most decisive differences among theological schools with regard to the way they assume their proper responsibility for spiritual formation have to do not with whether or not they are denominational or independent, free-standing or university-related, small or large, homogeneous or diverse in membership, but with the extent to which they understand their primary and indispensable mission to be theological education.

4

The Knowledge
Born of Obedience

"All right knowledge of God is born of obedience."[1] This claim of Calvin provokes some questions: How is obedience supposed to give rise to knowledge? What kind of knowledge, and specifically what kind of knowledge of God, is born of obedience? In what sense is this the "right" (*recta*) knowledge of God? What implications does this claim have for theological inquiry?

I want to propose a way of understanding the relationship between the knowledge of God and obedience, and then deal with what I take to be some implications of that relationship in the light of the understanding proposed. I will not claim that my understanding is particularly congruent with that of Calvin or any other theologian, only that it is an understanding that may help us see why some theologians have been led to offer theological explanations of the connection of knowledge to obedience. My account will not itself be properly theological, but philosophical, although it might have theological use.

That a right knowledge of God is born of obedience is not a conviction voiced by Calvin alone, although he expressed it with a helpful simplicity. It can be found throughout the Judaeo-Christian tradition, from those biblical passages that link knowing and right doing (for example, Jer. 9:1–6; 22:13–16; Hos. 4; John 7:17; 1 John 4:7–8) to the writings of Karl Barth and, still more recently, of various theologians of liberation.[2] The conviction is not the property of any single theological party or tendency, but is rather so pervasive that to dwell on any single instance is to run the risk of misrepresentation. In fact, the great variety of ways in which this relationship has been affirmed makes it more difficult to understand. Both "knowledge" and "obedience" have been so variously conceived, and their relationship pictured in such different ways, that it seems very difficult to establish any common ground for a discussion. For example, obedience may be equated with assent or belief, and then this assent or belief may be semantically promoted to the status of knowledge, it being understood that knowledge of the divine is a special case of knowledge so that ordinary strictures on the use of the concept do not apply. Or it may be held that the right knowledge of God is granted, by a special illumination, to those who believe or obey — a knowledge that is inaccessible to the unbeliever. The abundance of explanations is confusing; and the character of any of them, when scrutinized, may leave something to be desired.

There is an additional difficulty we may face in considering this subject, and that arises from the deep suspicion of any alleged dependence of knowledge upon obedience that we have as part of the legacy of the Enlightenment. On the whole it is a healthy and justifiable suspicion, and it should not in the least be set aside in this sort of inquiry. We are rightly suspicious of any suggestion that we should set aside our suspicions just this once. But if our suspicion leads us to a premature dismissal of a claim when in fact we have misunderstood the nature of the claim, then something has gone wrong. We have forgotten to suspect our own suspicion. The problem then is not that we have been too critical when the situation called for a softer or less rigorous approach, but that we have failed to be critical enough of our own assumptions and judgments.

In Kant's classic essay "What Is Enlightenment?," the immaturity in which most of us languish is described as "the incapacity to use one's intelligence without the guidance of another."[3] To "dare to know" is to dare to take one's leave of the authorities and tutors who would relieve one of the burden of thinking, and to begin to think for oneself. The "knowledge" a person has on authority, at second hand, is rightly suspect, perhaps even misnamed; real knowledge is what one can claim to have reached for oneself. Now, because "obedience" and "authority" are often connected in our thinking, it may seem from what Kant is saying that knowledge and obedience, so far from being related, are actually opposed: one may either seek knowledge or obey. The very possibility of a knowledge that comes *through* obedience is then inconceivable. If that is a correct statement of the situation, then perhaps the proper thing to do would be to expose "the knowledge born of obedience" as a devious honorific term for "opinion accepted on authority." But to take this course would be to misunderstand both Kant and Calvin in crucial respects. The burden of Kant's essay is to show that one may be an obedient servant of church and state in one's occupation and the "private" use of one's reason in that role, while at the same time pursuing the quest for enlightenment in one's scholarly inquiry and the "public" use of one's reason. Obedience does not require the renunciation of the freedom of thought; they are entirely compatible, in Kant's view. And although Calvin might differ sharply with Kant concerning the propriety and value of free inquiry — in some realms at least — his claim about knowledge and obedience seems in one important respect to exemplify Kant's principles rather than to violate them: One does not come to a right knowledge of God, in Calvin's view, by taking someone's word for it. One comes to know God by actually doing something, that is, by obeying. Obedience is not a substitute for knowledge, nor a way of getting over one's desire for knowledge, nor a way of convincing oneself of something. It is, simply, a way to knowledge; it is the route by which one may come to one's own knowledge of God. At least, that is what Calvin seems to claim.

That is why Calvin's particular formulation of the matter is helpful: it puts the stress on obedience, rather than, say, belief, as the path to knowledge. That is a significant decision. A person may obey without believing, just as a person may believe (in some sense of the word) without obeying. A person may take up a life of Christian obedience, for example, following the precepts of Jesus or of a church body, before he or she has come to accept the beliefs that normally accompany (and, we usually think, motivate) that way of life. Occasionally, such a course has actually been recommended to someone as a way of coming to belief: act as if you had faith and see what happens. Pascal's remarkable advice to the inquiring skeptic in his famous "Wager" in the *Pensées* is one notorious instance. Peter Boehler's advice to a doubtful and despairing John Wesley — "Preach faith till you have it and then because you have it, you will preach faith" — is another.[4] It is the behavior itself involved in obedience that seems important, as a guide, to both knowledge of God and faith.

Why is this so? A moment's consideration will reveal that there is nothing esoteric, and nothing peculiar to religious knowledge, about this state of affairs. It is not only in this realm that coming to know or extending one's knowledge requires that one engage in particular forms of behavior, and even that one practice a form of behavior and become habituated to it. The behavior enjoined may not make a great deal of sense at first. It is only later that one sees the point, whereas at the beginning one must simply be led or shown, put through the motions. This is not only true of our learning skills — learning to sail or learning a mathematical technique — but also of learning that is more clearly cognitive. Learning to make discriminating judgments is a matter involving "knowing" as well as "knowing how." Yet it is a knowledge one gains by experience, that is, by following certain forms of behavior that enable one to see what is there. What we apprehend in a situation depends a great deal on our bearing toward it, and that means not only what sort of interest we have in it (although that is important) but also what we are prepared to do with it. One person may dismiss the ink marks on a piece of paper as a meaningless scrawl or doodle, whereas another recognizes it as an unusual handwriting and proceeds to read it. My visit to the art gallery may profit me very little, whereas someone else, in less time and with less existential interest at the time, may acquire a great deal not only of enjoyment but of knowledge as well. With the help of a patient guide who was willing to point things out to me, to encourage and correct my attempts to understand, I might eventually come to learn more on subsequent visits.

It is vital to recognize that in cases such as these, a person is not simply picking up new forms of behavior or new words. One is also learning to see the world, and perhaps oneself too, in new ways. Behavior is not all that has been acquired. Rather, through the behavior one has also acquired a new knowledge of things. Words and concepts are not just labels we affix to realities already available to us; they are often the instruments through which we have access to those realities in the first place. And so to learn a concept (which, as Wittgenstein says, usually involves training and practice until one has it) is much more than to learn how to operate with some new words. It is to have access to a portion of the world that was previously closed off. It is often to extend one's ability to perceive as well as to act.

In this light, the advice of Pascal or Boehler becomes sensible. If one must become prepared, must have one's experience extended, one's existence qualified in certain ways, before one can apprehend what is in a situation, then it makes sense to recommend such training to someone who wants to acquire that apprehension. When Luther in his Preface to Romans cautioned his readers against proceeding to chapters 9–11 before they had thoroughly subjected themselves to the message of the earlier chapters, he was following the same course. "But you had better follow the order of this epistle," Luther wrote. "Worry first about Christ and the gospel, that you may recognize your sin and his grace. Then fight your sin, as the first eight chapters here have taught. Then, when you have reached the eighth chapter, and are under the cross and suffering, this will teach you correctly of predestination in chapters 9, 10, and 11, and how comforting it is. For in the absence of suffering and the cross and the perils of death, one cannot deal with predestination without harm and without secret anger against God. The old Adam must first die before he can tolerate this thing and drink the strong wine. Therefore beware that you do not drink wine while you are still a suckling. There is a limit, a time, and an age for every doctrine."[5]

Think of yourself and the world this way, Luther is saying — and do not simply entertain the possibility for a moment, but get accustomed to it, let it grow on you — *then* see what you see in this next part of the Epistle. Let your understanding be shaped by this material, and you will come to a different apprehension of things from the one you might otherwise have had.

Now, what Luther is advising here is not just a softening-up exercise, a procedure designed to weaken the reader's defenses and induce a credulous disposition. There are certain features of his approach that lend themselves to that interpretation, of course. We know that the more you are convinced of your own sinfulness, weakness, and stupidity, and the more anxious you become about all that, the more readily you may hear and accept the first solution that sounds promising without giving it the sort of critical scrutiny you might if you thought you had the time, the intelligence, and the moral right to examine it. You may find yourself giving wholehearted and grateful allegiance to propositions of dubious validity and disastrous implications, because their advocate has managed somehow to enlist your cooperation against yourself. There is a kind of evangelism that thrives on this approach, and it is not unknown in other fields of discourse.

It can still be maintained, I think, that Luther has not adopted this gambit here. He wants the readers of his exposition to be enlightened, not simply convinced. He is trying to enable them to see something so that they may believe rightly — in this case, to see what Paul's teaching on predestination is about so that they may find it a source of comfort and an aid to faith, rather than a provocation to secret anger against God. And Luther is aware that two things must happen if the necessary insight is to be gained: not only must the proper concepts be acquired, but, even before that can happen, barriers to understanding — here symbolized by the "old Adam" — must be overcome. It is vital here to recognize these as barriers to *understanding*. The old Adam may also be unwilling to believe, but it is his inability to apprehend which is the prior concern here. Understanding may require an extension of our experience, the acquisition of new abilities; but this in turn may require some changes in our present mode of living and thinking. That is, our current habits and practices may make it impossible for us to acquire a new concept — if only by depriving us of the time, energy, atmosphere, or concentration it takes to get hold of the concept. In any serious discussion of the conditions of knowledge, it is important not to overlook the sheer practical considerations that must be involved. In coming to know something, there are ordinarily procedures to be followed, operations to be performed, ways of attending to the data (and of making oneself attentive) that must be learned and implemented. Knowledge demands a discipline. And if a person's mode of life does not permit the requisite discipline, there is no shortcut.

It is sometimes held that there is an alternate route to the understanding of concepts of which one has had no prior experience, namely, through imagination. I need not actually be under the cross and suffering in order to understand predestination, according to this view; I can instead imagine that situation, picture what it would be like to be affected that way, and let that picture guide my understanding. I can entertain an experience just as I can entertain an idea, in order to assess its significance.

The fact that imagination has a role in human perception and understanding is generally acknowledged, although that role is variously conceived by different theorists. But there are several problems that would seem to count against the reliability of imagination as a path to the understanding of genuinely new concepts, if imagination is conceived simply as an alternative to experience. First, insofar as the acquisition of a new concept involves the extension of a person's experience into a new realm of activity or feeling or perceptivity, it is doubtful whether imagination in this sense is a useful guide. Imagination of this sort operates on the basis of prior experience: the key phrase we often use to initiate our imagining — "What would it be like to be or do *x?*" — betrays our reliance in imagination upon previous experience and knowledge. In what is here called "imagination" we are not actually extending our experience, but rather bringing past experience to bear upon a new situation, looking for precedents or analogies that will disclose the new situation to us and help us deal with it. And although some bizarre and apparently novel understandings may result from this recovery and recombination of elements of the past, it is basically incapable of genuine novelty. "I can calculate in the medium of imagination, but not experiment," wrote Wittgenstein, whose work contains several warnings against the notion that thought can really extend experience.[6]

Two other hazards associated with a reliance on imagination can be briefly mentioned. One is the fact that the activity of imagination is constrained not only by our history but also by our interests, our hopes and fears. The distrust of the imagination that appears from time to time in the biblical and Christian tradition — a distrust to which anti-intellectual or authoritarian motives are sometimes assigned — seems in most of its contexts to be based on a recognition of the ease with which our imagination is ruled by our self-interest, to the detriment of reason as well as of faith. Pascal's wry illustration comes to mind: "Put the world's greatest philosopher on a plank that is wider than need be: if there is a precipice below, although his reason may convince him that he is safe, his imagination will prevail. Many could not even stand the thought of it without going pale and breaking into sweat."[7]

The other hazard is the difficulty of exercising critical control over imagination. There are many things I cannot imagine, yet I may not be aware that I cannot imagine them. I may think I can imagine what it is like to be a yogin, or what it is to know God; but perhaps I cannot, because my experience does not provide any proper analogates. Yet because I can imagine *something* along that line, it may seem to me that I am imagining properly. Imagination does not know its own limits. We are accustomed, in certain moods anyway, to think of imagination or fantasy as a perfectly free medium in which we can roam at will and nothing is alien to us. But this freedom to render the alien familiar is itself imaginary in those crucial instances when we confront a concept or a reality that hitherto has been truly outside our experience. Here, something like a conversion of the intellect seems to be called for — that is, a recognition of the insufficiency of present understanding and a willingness to be led toward a new understanding.[8]

A more adequate account of imagination, of course, would acknowledge its own experiential base, that is, the rootage of image-formation in activity. There is a sense in which one's inquiring participation in a new mode of life, religious or otherwise, is properly termed an imaginative venture: new experiences are giving rise to new images and symbols or are making standard ones freshly available for appropriation. Such an account of imagination would relate imagination and conceptual formation closely, but precisely by stressing the behavioral or experiential foundations of both. It would still be important not to equate the two or to link them inextricably together. Surely conceptualization is not always bound to image-formation. In any case, the fairly common notion of imagination as a substitute for experience simply does not do justice to the complex relationship between imagination and understanding. But because it is common and has been invoked all too often in the interpretation of religion, it is well to rule it out explicitly from the obediential approach to knowledge being discussed here.

What kind of knowledge is born of obedience? The best general characterization for it might be the term "apprehension." It is a more immediate knowledge than that gained through inference or discursive procedure generally. Its acquisition does not so much involve operations upon the data as it involves operations upon the knower. Through obedience, a person undergoes the kind of training, refining, equipping, and positioning of the self that enables one to apprehend. One is "brought to" the data in a new way, able to receive it afresh. Metaphors derived from sense perception, and especially from sight, spring readily into use. "Now I see!" What one has is not simply knowledge of a new concept, but knowledge *through* a new concept: that is, one gains a concept by being trained in it, and then through the concept one has access to certain features of reality. It is as if the new concept gives one a new sensation, as Wittgenstein once remarked.[9] One could almost say that concepts are organs by means of which we have access to the world.

The use of the language of sensory apprehension in connection with the knowledge of God is fairly common in the Christian tradition and has been given particular development by several writers.

The "sense of the heart" in Jonathan Edwards is a notable example. John Wesley provides another. When Wesley speaks of faith as a "spiritual sensation" whereby a person "discerneth God and the things of God," he compares it to the activity of several senses. It is "the eye of the newborn soul" that sees God, "the ear of the soul" hearing the message of the forgiveness of sins, "the palate of the soul" tasting the good word, "the feeling of the soul" perceiving the presence, power, and love of God.[10] The new birth, for Wesley, involves the acquisition of this new sensorium of the soul, and he uses the language of sense perception — especially of seeing — in a disconcertingly straightforward way. The reborn soul has a capacity for seeing God in the world, and the world in God, which the unregenerate lacks.

But what sort of difference is this? Is the believer really able to "see" something the nonbeliever cannot? Or is it simply that the believer is inclined to interpret things differently or to read some assumptions into the evidence?[11] An understanding of the relationship of knowledge to the sort of experience involved in "obedience" may throw light on this issue. Fundamentally, the difference between two people who observe the same situation and apprehend it differently might best be understood in some cases as a difference in their repertory of concepts. One of them is actually able to discern more in the situation than the other is, because the first has acquired, through appropriate experience, the sort of conceptual background that permits a fuller reading of the evidence. They do not simply have different views of the situation, they have different *visions* of it. They are not simply inclined toward different interpretations or predisposed to them by their divergent beliefs and attitudes; rather, one of them is able to make use of the evidence in a way the other cannot. They have different abilities or capacities with regard to the situation. In short, it is the believer's obediential experience (obedience which may, of course, be theologically understood as enabled by grace) that leads to the apprehension of God.

There are uses of the term "knowledge" in which what I have been calling "apprehension" would have a fairly low status. According to these uses, knowing involves some degree of reflection and of intentionality, and is not nearly so immediate and so passive as "apprehension" generally connotes. Knowing, as Bernard Lonergan rightly observes, "is not just seeing; it is experiencing, understanding, judging, and believing."[12] This means that my claim to know something on the basis of my apprehension in a given situation is not a self-validating or indisputable claim. I may mistake what I apprehend; I may be moved to make unwarranted claims about it. Thus, even if I manage through patient guidance and nurture to lead someone to share my apprehension in a situation, that person may still not share my judgment. To say that the knowledge of God is born of obedience — that it has its origin in one's subjection to a particular regimen of thought, feeling, and action — is not necessarily to say that the knowledge claimed on this basis needs no further justification or defense. To claim that all *right* knowledge of God has its origin in obedience — at least, as I have construed this claim — is just to claim, first, that it is through obedience, through deliberate practice, that one acquires the capacities that permit the sort of apprehension of reality that one may want to call an apprehension of God; and second, that this apprehension, or direct acquaintance, is somehow the most basic or fitting or appropriate knowledge of God for a person to have.

But because apprehension is neither judgment nor a substitute for judgment, there is still ample room for discussion concerning the meaning and significance of what has been apprehended.

5

Finding the Life of a Text

Notes on the Explication of Scripture

Some form of our familiar distinction between letter and spirit in the interpretation of a text is surely older than written language itself. Whenever understanding becomes problematic — and this includes not only instances when an utterance is opaque or ambiguous, but also those frequent instances in which the obvious meaning of an utterance is not its intended meaning — this distinction may come into play as a way of attacking the problem. We find the distinction useful in our ordinary conversation with one another, when we are trying to decide how to take what someone has just said to us: "I know what he said, but how did he mean it? What was the spirit of what he said?" In irony, sarcasm, understatement, allusion, and other devices of our common speech, there is often considerable divergence between the letter and the spirit of the utterance or between what is said and what is meant. These distinctions were not invented by hermeneuticians trying to rationalize the devious interpretations to which canonical literatures are sometimes subjected. They have grown up with our language.

Of course, these primary distinctions have been developed in some interesting ways by the interpreters of sacred texts and by those who reflect on such interpretations. The developments have usually been prompted by some prior need or interest. The Christian fathers who found certain Old Testament passages offensive could use the letter-spirit distinction to bring out an edifying dimension in such passages, using, as did countless successors, the Pauline sanction: "the letter kills, but the spirit gives life" (2 Cor. 3:6). The medieval elaboration of the multiple senses of scripture rests upon this more elementary separation of meaning from text. Even though the various spiritual senses of a text were theoretically subordinate to the literal sense, in practice a text could have several valid meanings with no clear order of priority among them.

When the mature Luther repudiated this tradition of interpretation and bound meaning to verbal sense, he did so in such a way as to preserve the letter-spirit distinction in a form that was to have great influence on subsequent hermeneutical thought. For Luther, there was not a spiritual sense in addition to a valid literal sense in a scriptural text; rather, the spiritual sense was the literal sense correctly understood. To read the text with understanding is to perceive the Spirit, for it is the Spirit who grants understanding. Apart from the Spirit, the letter is mere words and signs. We might say that for Luther, the operative distinction was not between various possible "understandings" of a text, but rather between understanding the text and merely reading the words. The living text is the text as understood in the Spirit; at the same time, there is no understanding apart from verbal sense.

To Luther, the spirit of the text was, of course, the Holy Spirit. He was concerned with the sacred text and did not extend his hermeneutical reflection to secular literature — although he did consider the letter-spirit paradigm valid for some post-biblical Christian writing. It remained for a later thinker to restate Luther's position in nontheological categories and to do so in a way that was to set the course of modern interpretation theory. This was the eighteenth-century philosopher Christian Wolff. Wolff's strength was not his originality, but his ability to set forth a total world-picture in a coherent and persuasive form. It was this that made him one of the principal architects of the emerging modern consciousness. In his history of the background of modern hermeneutics, *The Eclipse of Biblical Narrative,* Hans Frei traces the impact of Wolff upon later biblical interpretation.[1] That impact is largely the result of Wolff's version of the letter-spirit distinction.

According to Wolff, there are two ways in which an unfamiliar concept may be interpreted: verbal explanation (*Worterklärung*) involves listing some of the distinguishing characteristics of the concept (it tells us what sort of thing it is), whereas subject-matter explanation (*Sacherklärung*) shows how the object signified by the concept is possible. *Worterklärung* gives us other words for the concept. *Sacherklärung* introduces us to the object behind the concept. To appreciate the force of the distinction, it helps to know that in Wolff's theory of knowledge, we know something only through experience or through proof. "Experience" means direct, personal verification of its being so. "Proof" means the demonstration of its possibility (that is, an account of how the thing comes to be) or of its implication in something already known.[2] Words are the signs of thoughts, and thoughts represent objects. To understand a concept, then, is to know the object to which it refers. If we do not know the object, no amount of verbal explanation will help us. Although verbal explanation is sometimes useful, as in helping us to recognize an object we already know under another name, it is clearly subordinate to subject-matter explanation. Mere words are useless if we do not know that to which they refer.

Thus Luther's form of the letter-spirit distinction was given new life as a letter–subject-matter distinction. One who reads with understanding grasps the subject matter of what is read. (And at the same time, it is the reader's prior grasp of the subject matter that permits understanding in the first place. This is the Wolffian form of the hermeneutical circle.) One who reads without penetrating to the *Sache* simply misses the point. All the familiar metaphors of earlier ages, such as shell and kernel, husk and heart, could be revived in speaking of the relationship of words and meaning.

This new account of understanding appealed to a general theory of the nature of human knowledge, and not to a privileged theological standpoint, for its support. It is not the illuminating influence of the Holy Spirit, but the penetrating power of human knowledge, that discerns the meaning in the mute text and permits understanding. The content of that understanding was different also. For Wolff, and for the age whose sensibility he helped to shape, to understand something is to understand the conditions of its possibility. An explanation of something is adequate only when it gives an account of how the thing comes to be. To understand a machine, for example, it is not enough to know what it is for; we must know how it is made, how it is put together to do what it does. To understand a religious text, it is not enough to know "what it says," on the surface, as it were; we must discover what it is in human nature or human experience which has given rise to that sort of utterance. We must know the circumstances of its production in order to discover to what it really refers. It is in this way that living meaning can be extracted from a text, as we go beyond mere verbal interpretation to an understanding of what the text actually represents, its true subject matter. Whether this subject matter turns out to be an experience of the Holy, a historical event of some kind, an ideal struggling for expression, or an object of some other sort, it is this that the interpreter must seek if an adequate interpretation of the text is to be achieved.

Obviously, such a course of interpretation is likely to be much less closely bound to the verbal sense of the text than was Luther's. This freedom from literalistic reading was seen as a positive achievement by Wolff's theological followers. The Bible came to be regarded as the *source* of revelation, rather than as a revealed text. That is, it is the subject matter of the text rather than the text itself that bears religious significance.[3]

This way of looking at religious texts has been enormously influential not only in modern theology but in religious studies as well, and is assumed in several current approaches to interpretation. That is, it is commonly assumed that the interpreter's first major task is somehow to isolate and identify the subject matter of the text — its *raison d'être,* its point, the central phenomenon from which it takes its life — so that the various elements of the text can be related to that center and understood in its light. The interpreter can thus give proper emphasis to those features of the text that illuminate and are illuminated by the subject matter and can properly dispose of the less illuminating residue. The quest for the subject matter of a text can be undertaken in many different ways, as in existentialist, structuralist, phenomenological, psychoanalytic, and socio-political approaches. Each of these is seen by its advocates as a means of recovering the spirit from the letter, of finding and freeing the life of the text.

There is something perennially fascinating about this problem of letter and spirit, of words and meaning. How does an utterance manage to mean, to communicate? We know that it does, or that at any rate it can, but how does it happen? How do we get from the noises or marks we call words to an understood meaning? Since the beginning of the nineteenth century, hermeneutical theorists have tended to study the phenomenon of understanding itself in their search for an answer. It is what goes on within the reader that converts the mute text into living meaning. Schleiermacher set the tone for this approach when he asserted that hermeneutics is concerned only with the *ars intelligendi,* the art of understanding, and not with the *ars explicandi,* the art of explication, though the two had coexisted in earlier hermeneutics. For Schleiermacher, explication is actually the creation of a new text, which in turn must be understood.[4] Explication is in effect a falling away from the primal phenomenon of understanding, in which the spirit of the utterance is grasped. To explicate is to attempt once again to embody the spirit in language; it involves the interpreter in all the ambiguities and tensions of the creative act itself. And the result is another frozen expression of what the understanding had perceived as living meaning. The problematic relationship of language and understanding has continued to dominate hermeneutical discussion to the present, as another incarnation of the letter-spirit question.

Ludwig Wittgenstein wrote: "Every sign *by itself* seems dead. *What* gives it life? — In use it is *alive*. Is life breathed into it there? — Or is the *use* its life?"[5] This query represents Wittgenstein's own approach to this subject, an approach that differs significantly from that of the main hermeneutical tradition. Wittgenstein suggests that we might look for the life of an utterance, not "in the understanding," but in its use. Those familiar with Wittgenstein's treatments of such concepts as meaning, intending, expecting, knowing, and understanding know that he tried to break the hold upon us of certain images suggested by these terms, so that we could more readily appreciate their actual functioning in our language. An approach like his might have some value in our search for the life of a text.

Language works because it is a collection of loosely related, shared conventions. I understand what you say, because we agree in our use of words. I may or may not agree with what you say, but our participation in the same linguistic conventions enables me to understand you. If I do not immediately understand, you can lead me by one means or another until I do. If someone speaks to me in Arabic, I will not understand at all because I do not share those conventions. Language lives in its use. We do not ordinarily think of words as mere noises or marks on paper, because we are absorbed in their use. Our linguistic experience provides a context within which the words live. It is when we are confronted with an utterance in isolation from any enlightening context — when the sign is by itself, as Wittgenstein says — that it seems dead. A phrase in an unknown language, or even in English, uttered apart from any indication of its use, is letter without spirit.

But that is an extreme example. The letter-spirit distinction usually comes into play when conventions are being stretched somehow or are found inadequate to deal with an utterance. If you say, "It's raining," I would ordinarily understand you. If you make that remark while we are standing under a sunny sky, I might ask you what you mean. If you reply, "I mean, it's raining back home," and I know you have just been on the telephone, then I may be satisfied that I understand. But if you say, "It's raining on the moon," and you are serious, then it may require a good deal more elucidation, because I do not know how to take such an utterance.

Like any ordinary utterance, a scriptural text lives in its use. So long as its use is supported by a network of conventions, so that everybody knows what it means or knows how to find out, interpretation does not become a serious problem. But sometimes these conventions break down or are challenged. What was formerly taken as the obvious meaning of a scriptural passage may now be seen as morally or theologically offensive or simply as incredible. Yet the passage is scriptural and cannot be unwritten. The task is then to decide how the passage is to be taken, how its "real" meaning is discerned. At such times of changing sensibility in a culture or religious community, the question of the relation of letter and spirit or of language and meaning becomes more than a fascinating philosophical problem. The situation of the early Christian interpreters of Hebrew scriptures is one sort of example. The situation of many theologians of Wolff's generation is another. Without denying the authority of the scripture, both groups had to get around what had seemed to be the obvious meaning of certain parts of the text, because that meaning was no longer admissible. To put it more accurately, their wish to affirm the authority of the scripture was what made a reinterpretation necessary, for they could no longer accept some of the implications of the text. The old conventions were no longer secure. The old meanings were no longer completely credible. Changing assumptions demanded the relocation of the "real" meaning of the text, so that the text could continue to function. Similar crises have been faced by other faith communities in their dealings with a canonical text during a period of change.

This is not to suggest that such relocated or respecified meaning is contrived or illegitimate. In the first place, the interpreter may not have a conscious choice. Granted the prevailing criteria for meaning and truth, the text simply must be interpreted in this way; it is the only way open, and it seems natural and obvious. The new approach is as compelling, logically and psychologically, for its followers as the old approach was in its time. In the second place, the new line of interpretation may actually be more nearly valid than the old. An interpretation regarded as secure for generations may nonetheless be quite inadequate. Sometimes it takes a crisis to open up a new and valuable perspective on a text, when tradition has had too firm a grip on its readers.

To use such words as "valid" and "adequate" in connection with interpretation implies that there are criteria for evaluating interpretations and judging their success. We are less inclined than some periods have been to assume that there is always only one correct interpretation of a text. We admit a plurality of interpretations, depending upon the assumptions and the aims of the readers, and we find that differing perspectives may yield complementary rather than strictly conflicting interpretations. We are skeptical when someone ventures to tell us what a text "really means"; we want to know by what standards this proffered meaning is adjudged more real or more adequate than another. We do not find ourselves condemned to relativism, but we know that there are choices to be made and that these decisions need to be justified. A text may be put to many uses. Interpreters are more and more being pressed to defend their uses on various grounds — theological and ethical as well as philosophical.

Since the time of Wolff, interpreters and hermeneuticians have appealed to a general theory of knowledge or of understanding to make such defense unnecessary. True understanding, this tradition tells us, is the process that faithfully captures the authentic meaning of the text. Through understanding, the text is allowed to speak for itself; it is understood on its own terms. Understanding was sometimes distinguished from explanation, in which a text is read in terms of some alien standard or framework and distorted to fit the categories the reader wants to impose upon it. Understanding, by contrast, preserves the integrity and autonomy of the text.

The distinction between understanding and explication supports this prior claim of the text: any explication is likely to be a limited, partial representation of what a given text means and must be kept subordinate to the text itself and to the process of understanding in which the textual meaning is realized. Often, no single explication can do full justice to a text. A successful explication is not a substitute for the text but an instrument through which the interpreter may help another to understand the text.

This insistence upon the integrity of the text, its right to be heard in its own terms, is one of the most valuable legacies of the modern hermeneutical tradition. But the attempt to protect that integrity by positing a special process of understanding, a special way of knowing, can no longer be sustained.

Interpretation is an activity. The meaning of a text is always construed, however subconsciously. The text does not simply mean something; we take it to mean something, we draw meaning from it. In our ordinary reading and conversation, this is a seemingly effortless activity, because the conventions upon which we rely are so familiar and well established. We even have conventions for the unconventional uses of language. Nonetheless, it is by drawing implications that we come to understand. That this is the case may be seen much more readily when we are dealing with a difficult utterance — say, a centuries-old religious text from another culture. We immediately begin to try out meanings, to test the tentative implications we have drawn against whatever criteria we recognize. We look for confirmation or correction. We do not assume that our first or easiest construction is correct. In fact, we learn to distrust our inclination to assign meanings. We learn to be cautious in accepting what seems to be obvious. By working at explicating the text and trying out our hypotheses, we become familiar, over a period of time, with the conventions governing this body of writing. We gradually acquire the ability to follow the meaning, to anticipate the next step in an argument or the next development in a narrative, and to draw appropriate conclusions from the text. These and similar abilities constitute our understanding of the material. That is, someone who exercises such abilities consistently is generally said to understand the text.

This is not to say that understanding is to be equated with the performance of certain mechanical operations upon and with an utterance or a document. One reason for the strong appeal of the "inner process" model of understanding is that understanding has to do with learning linguistic conventions, and these are not external or superficial, but deep within human life. To understand is to master these conventions to such a degree that we sense the coherence, the fitness, of what is said. We follow it; we sense why one part follows another, why the elements of the text fit together as they do. The text makes sense to us. This internalized grasp of conventions is, in most cases, an integral part of understanding — not because understanding is finally a subjective state, but because genuine mastery of a text generally demands that sort of familiarity with its life.

Understanding is gained, strengthened, exercised, and demonstrated through that collection of activities we call explication. Schleiermacher's distinction between understanding and explication, despite its obvious value and despite Schleiermacher's own intention, is finally misleading, because it suggests a false distance between them. It suggests that an interpreter first comes to understand an utterance and then explicates it. Explication is seen as the restatement, re-presenting, re-creation in other terms of what has been understood. But in fact we come to understand only by explicating ("unfolding") what is implicit in the text. It is by tracing the implications of what is being said, tracing them through and beyond the text, that we discover how the language is being used. It is in explication that we find the life of the text. Explication, then, is not the anticlimactic result of our understanding, but the very means by which that understanding is acquired. It would clarify our own real interests considerably, therefore, if we were to shift our hermeneutical focus from the theoretical problem of understanding to the actual problems of explication. We need to recognize that our problem of understanding is actually a collection of problems having to do with explication, and that these problems vary with the sort of material under consideration. How are meanings to be construed and validated? What criteria of understanding are appropriate in a given case? Whose use of the text is to be taken as normative? What interpretative approaches are likely to be most helpful? Questions such as these are the proper concern of hermeneutics. They need to be addressed in both general and specific contexts.

When the conventions supporting the use of a text are weakened or destroyed, the text itself seems endangered, if not dead. It is not simply its claim to truth that is threatened, but its very meaning. People no longer know how to take it, what sense to make of it. Writings that function as scripture over a period of centuries may experience this crisis many times. Each time, the question of letter and spirit, language and meaning, may be raised again, though perhaps never twice in just the same way. Both the Wolffian-inspired search for the subject matter of scripture and the later hermeneutical preoccupation with the event of understanding were powerful attempts within our own modern cultural history to rediscover and relocate the life of such texts. They were powerful because each in its own way freed the text from its interpretative tradition and related it to newly emerging criteria of explanation. But perhaps that liberation from the traditional context of interpretation, in deference to new standards of meaningfulness, was too complete. The cumulative effect of these hermeneutical efforts seems to have been to separate meaning more and more from the text it was supposed to enliven, as the text becomes an archaic source of religious or anthropological data rather than a functioning instrument in the life of an individual, community, or culture. A scriptural text, like any other utterance, lives in its use. Luther's insight was essentially correct: the Spirit is the letter understood. That understanding is achieved through patient and thorough explication. It is when hermeneutics directs us to that task and provides us with resources for the explication of scripture that it helps us to encounter a living text.

6

Hermeneutics and the Authority of Scripture

What bearing, if any, ought the fact that a given text or body of texts is "scripture," that is, authoritative writing, to have upon the principles governing its interpretation? Two opposing answers to this question — one typically "liberal," the other typically "conservative" — come readily to mind. According to the first, the fact that texts have authoritative status within a religious community ought to have no bearing at all upon their interpretation. There should be no "sacred hermeneutics," no privilege given these texts on account of their supposed authority; they should be treated like any other. Of course, the fact that they are *religious* texts may indicate that they should be approached with the resources of a particular "regional" hermeneutics, just as texts of other sorts may require their own particular hermeneutical considerations. But valid interpretation requires that one disregard the ways in which the community or communities for which these texts are "scripture" have described and approached them as such. The interpreter who happens to be a member of such a community must also prescind from any consideration of the authority of these texts for his or her own life and must approach them as free as possible from any prior commitment to their normativeness. Only thus will the texts be able to speak for themselves rather than being made to say something that corresponds to the interpreter's dogmatic preunderstanding. On this view, giving questions of scriptural authority any role in hermeneutics is a sure way to subvert the aims of interpretation. The question of what authority these texts should possess can be taken up *after* interpretation, if at all — certainly not before.

According to the opposing view, a prior commitment to the authority of the scriptural text is the only way to a proper understanding of it. The text functions to disclose or to teach something that may not be otherwise accessible to us and that we are not predisposed to receive. If we approach it as we would other materials, subjecting it to scrutiny and testing by our ordinary reason and experience, we will only miss its message, because that message transcends our ordinary reason and experience. The interpreter must submit to the text, accepting its authority and being instructed and shaped by it, if he or she is to understand it. Scripture should not be treated like any other writing, because it is not like any other writing. (The advocate of this view is ordinarily a member of a particular community, and it is that community's scripture, and not sacred writings in general, that he or she has in mind when making such claims. But one might envision a more generic version of this position, in which it is claimed that any religious text can only be understood by an insider to its community.) Furthermore, that prior commitment to the authority of the text must be of the right sort: we must understand what this text is and how it is authoritative before we will know how to submit our understanding to it. In other words, a proper doctrine of the authority of scripture — a doctrine derived, perhaps, from scripture itself or from some other authorized source in the community (a magisterium) — is the necessary precondition for valid interpretation and must have a prominent role in hermeneutical reflection.

The adherents of each of these views are understandably suspicious of the adherents of the other. From the standpoint of the first answer, those who advocate the second wrongly allow extrinsic considerations (for example, a particular community's judgments concerning the nature and content of a text) to determine their understanding of it, rather than letting the text speak for itself. Further, they tend to hold confused or mistaken ideas concerning judgments of truth — perhaps maintaining, in precritical fashion, that one may simply assume the truth of what scripture teaches, or perhaps offering some sort of fideistic view according to which there can be no appeal to truth-criteria beyond the circle of faith constituted by a given community's relation to its scripture. From the standpoint of the second answer, the advocates of the first view are simply imposing their own authority upon the text, under the guise of a freedom from dogmatic constraints. By disregarding the scriptural status and context of a given text, they are refusing to let it be what it is. Further, they do not recognize that their refusal to take seriously the normative character of the text gives an unwarranted normativity to their own standards of reasonableness, meaningfulness, and truth, and does not allow these standards to be challenged and corrected by what the text has to say.

Recent hermeneutical developments have led to refinements of these two opposing positions and to some attempts to mediate between them. Nevertheless, they remain effectively in place. Like some political positions, each is sustained by a sort of coalition of interests, and differences within each coalition can threaten the stability and coherence of the position. (Currently, for example, fundamentalists and liberation theologians may find themselves uneasily allied in criticizing certain aspects of the "liberal" position, and liberals may find some of their own arguments against the "conservative" position co-opted by neoconservatives who apply them to liberation theologians.) But despite the shakiness of the coalitions holding at any given time, the positions have an inherent power because each embodies certain valid insights.

My aim in this chapter is to propose and defend an answer to our opening question that combines the strengths of these two opposing positions while avoiding their weaknesses. I hope to show that the scriptural status of texts is hermeneutically relevant for certain purposes and that a doctrine of the authority of scripture may have a proper hermeneutical function. At the same time, I will argue that an acknowledgment of these points is eminently compatible with an insistence that the questions of the meaning and truth of scriptural texts not be begged. The answer will be worked out here specifically in terms of Christian scripture; *mutatis mutandis,* it might be applicable to scriptures in other traditions.

Nonscriptural Uses of Scripture

Scripture is writing that is authoritative for some community. As David Kelsey puts it, " 'Authoritative' is part of the meaning of 'scripture' "; the notion of authority is analytic in the concept of scripture.[1] Of course, the fact that scripture is authoritative for a community does not mean that it must be regarded as authoritative by its interpreters or that it must be interpreted as an authoritative text. Interpreters within or outside the community whose scripture it is may for various reasons disregard its authority — that is, disregard its character as scripture — on the grounds that for their particular purposes its authoritative character is either irrelevant or inadmissible. Historians of early Christianity, for example, are obliged to treat the texts of the New Testament as ordinary historical documents, neither more nor less reliable in principle than noncanonical texts as sources for historical investigation. The authority ascribed to New Testament texts by the Christian community has no bearing upon their historical reliability. (At the same time, the fact that the church has ascribed authority to certain texts, has preserved them, given them prominence, traditionally trusted them as historical records, and so on, is a fact of great historical significance that the historian must take into account — not because it is evidence for the texts' historical authenticity but because it helps to explain such things as the state of the documentation for the early Christian movement.) Scriptural texts may also be put to other uses for which their scriptural status is irrelevant: they may, for example, be studied for their literary value, or analyzed as examples of Hebrew or Greek syntax, or combed for interesting vignettes of human behavior.

Among the nonscriptural uses of scripture are some that we may call (for lack of a better term) *religious* uses. These are uses of scriptural texts in which their potential claim upon the life of their users is taken seriously but in which the text is regarded more as a resource than as an authority. Text and reader are in principle on the same level here. The reader is open to the text's influence and may well be affected, even deeply, by it; but the reader is also free to criticize and transcend the text. It is a resource, perhaps of great significance, but it is not a norm. Interpretation is a dialogue or conversation or (less irenically put) a struggle with the text, the desired outcome of which is not the reader's submission to or conformation with the text but rather the realization of some new insight or value beyond what the text itself contains — a new stage in the growth of the tradition in which both text and reader stand.

Elisabeth Schüssler Fiorenza frequently uses the contrast between "archetype" and "prototype" in advocating her own version of this nonauthoritative use of biblical texts: an archetype is a normative pattern, any deviation from which is an error; a prototype is a first attempt, from which one may learn both positively and negatively, and which may and probably should be surpassed.[2] In associating biblical texts with the latter rather than with the former concept, Schüssler Fiorenza means in effect to reject the notion of

Christian scripture, that is, of authoritative texts. Her canon is an extrabiblical one — the liberation of women, as that is defined in the struggle for liberation itself.[3]

Another recent exponent of this sort of use of scripture is Delwin Brown. He proposes a redefinition rather than a relocation of theological authority, but in doing so he uses a pair of contrasting concepts that are instructively similar in function to those used by Schüssler Fiorenza: he rejects an "authorization" model in favor of an "authoring" model of biblical authority. The Bible does not serve as a norm authorizing theological proposals; it serves as a source that "authors" new life, giving its readers the power and freedom to realize new possibilities for existence. The text is powerful and empowering, but it is not normative. The conservatism of the authorization model, which binds us to a standard frozen in the past, must be overcome in favor of a model that opens us to novelty in the future.[4]

For both Brown and Schüssler Fiorenza, the texts of Christian scripture are best viewed as portions of tradition to which the community, for a mixture of reasons (not altogether creditable), has given normative status. If this bestowal of status were simply a way of acknowledging the superior natural life-giving or liberating power of the texts relative to other portions of the tradition, it might be regarded as benign in intention. But insofar as it involves an attempt by the community (or, more accurately, by some segments of the community) to establish standards for belief and conduct and thus to set limits to the community's creative freedom with the tradition, it must be viewed with suspicion. Schüssler Fiorenza emphasizes the ways in which the formation of the New Testament involved the legitimizing of certain (especially sexist) interests and thus represented an ideological victory for cultural norms over the egalitarian tendencies of primitive Christianity. Brown argues that the very notion of normative tradition has no valid place in Christianity: to identify a standard in the past to which Christians are expected always to conform is to renounce that God-given creative freedom in which the tradition is summoned constantly to transcend itself so that human potential may be more fully realized. In any case, the church's ways of ascribing particular authority to these texts — of marking them off from ordinary tradition, rationalizing their status, and making them, in some sort of unity, the criterion for Christian faith and life — should have no bearing upon their interpretation. Valid interpretation requires an original and critical encounter with the texts in themselves, in which their own power and also their limitations may be discerned. The church's judgments about these texts — that is, doctrines of the authority of scripture — are at best irrelevant to this sort of encounter.

Though I have focused here upon two recent advocates of the view that a nonscriptural approach to scriptural texts is theologically appropriate, the general position is widely shared. A good many contemporary theologians would acknowledge that the texts of Christian scripture have had a special role in the formation and maintenance of the Christian tradition and that they are therefore particularly worthy of attention if one is attempting to understand the substance and dynamics of that tradition. But, these theologians would argue, to take them as authoritative (that is, normative) is unwarranted. At the beginning of this chapter, I characterized this as a typically liberal response, because it has often been ingredient in treatments of theological authority developed in liberal theology — for example, the relocation of theological authority from "holy scripture" to the life and teachings of the historical Jesus or to some immanent principle of religious or cultural evolution, or the renunciation of the very notion of authority as incompatible with enlightened or responsible faith. For such positions, the concept of authoritative text or scripture as such is one with no place in serious theology, and one the church as a whole may in good time outgrow. In short, from this standpoint, the fact that these writings are regarded as scripture by a community ought to have no bearing on their interpretation, because this very designation is at best an anachronism, and one of the positive tasks of hermeneutics is to enable the community to overcome the unfortunate relationship to its texts that the designation "scripture" represents and to find or recover a more appropriate one.

Hermeneutical Implications of Scriptural Status

On the other hand, those who affirm rather than lament the scriptural status of biblical texts generally take this status to be hermeneutically significant. That is, where the texts are regarded not simply as a sample of early tradition, but as the *criterion* of tradition — as tradition that is somehow distinctively authoritative — this regard is normally (and rightly) thought to have hermeneutical implications. Although this position is for obvious reasons generally typical of conservative theologies, it is not found exclusively there and can in fact be developed in quite other directions. It is intrinsically conservative only in the formal sense that a historically prior reality (scripture) is given some sort of normative status over subsequent developments; but, as Christian history has repeatedly shown, this conservatism can have radical consequences. To call something "scripture" is to affirm a critical principle: it is to identify something over against "tradition" (even if it is also *within* tradition) by which the authenticity of tradition may be evaluated and by which the development of tradition may be guided. It is to remove the presumption — which may be more characteristic of a conventionally conservative outlook — that tradition per se is valid and to put in its place the principle that tradition must be tested.

Our concern in this chapter is not to determine whether or not the texts constituting the Christian Bible — or, for that matter, any texts at all — ought to be regarded as scripture by the Christian church or ought to function in any authoritative way in Christian theology. Rather, assuming their authority, our purpose is to ask whether that status has any proper bearing upon their interpretation. Characteristically, those who answer this question in the negative also deny — explicitly or implicitly — that very assumption; that is, they typically claim that the texts ought not to be regarded as authoritative. Instead, they are to be treated as resources of one sort or another. Such positions are at least consistent in this regard. It would be inconsistent to affirm or assume the scriptural status of the texts and to deny that the status has hermeneutical implications. What sort of implications it has is what we must now investigate.

Ascribing authority to texts involves making certain judgments about them. Any well-developed normative account of the authority of scripture will make these judgments explicit by furnishing answers to three principal questions. First, for what is this material authoritative? Second, how does it exercise its authority? Third, why is it authoritative? The first question concerns the scope of scripture's authority; the second, its character; and the third, its source. The same questions might be addressed by a descriptive account of scripture's authority for a community — an account of what is sometimes called its *de facto* authority. In that case, attention of a social-scientific sort would be given to the actual functioning of scriptural authority in the community — its scope, its character, its source. Here, however, the concern is with a normative account, or a doctrine, of the authority of scripture, or with what can be called its *de jure* authority: What is the *proper* scope of scripture's authority? How *should* it function authoritatively? *Why* is it authoritative? What it means to take a particular body of texts as scripture depends upon the answers given to these questions.

For example, demarcations of the scope of scriptural authority have varied widely. Some have held that scripture is authoritative on any subject insofar as a passage from scripture may be taken to convey any information about that subject. Scripture is then the final arbiter, in principle, on any question, whether of history, geology, cosmology, anthropology, or grammar, on which some part of scripture may touch. Others have made a distinction between what scripture happens to contain and what it teaches, and have restricted the scope of scriptural authority to the latter — often further specified as matters concerning faith and morals, as distinct (it may be) from history or natural science. (Of course, it may also be held that certain historical or scientific beliefs are matters of faith, in which case the scope of scriptural authority extends to these things. This claim, then, like the first position mentioned, raises questions concerning the relationship between such historical or scientific beliefs and critical scholarship in these fields, and, more generally, questions concerning the relationship of biblical authority to secular inquiry, of faith to knowledge, and so on.)

The scope of scriptural authority has sometimes been further demarcated not with respect to the sorts of beliefs or activities upon which its authority bears but rather with respect to the sort of validity that may be adjudged by an appeal to scripture. It is widely held in contemporary theology that there are at least two basic questions, of different sorts, that theological reflection is obliged to raise concerning the validity of any instance of Christian witness: there is the question of its faithfulness to normative Christianity (what Schubert M. Ogden calls its "appropriateness," and David H. Kelsey its "Christianness"), and there is the question of its meaningfulness and truth. Those who make such a distinction frequently go on to affirm that although scriptural authority may bear upon the first of these questions, it cannot bear upon the second. That is, one may appeal to scripture to settle the question of whether a given stance is authentically Christian, but not to settle the question of whether it is credible or true.[5]

Such decisions concerning the scope of scriptural authority, particularly as they are made more specific, are inevitably bound up with other judgments concerning both the character and the source of that authority. To say that scripture is authoritative in what it teaches concerning faith and morals, for instance, is to suggest a range of ways in which the character of its authority — that is, how it functions authoritatively — might be conceived. If the accent is on the *fides quae creditur,* scripture's authority will most likely be conceived in doctrinal terms: for example, scripture will be conceived to function as the repository of, or guide to, right doctrine. If the accent is rather on the *fides qua creditur,* attention might instead be concentrated on the ways in which scripture functions to evoke and shape faithful dispositions. Scripture as *teacher* rather than as *teachings* might be the motif, and the effects of scripture upon its readers or hearers, rather than its cognitive content, might be highlighted.

Similarly, certain accounts of the source of scriptural authority will comport more naturally with some options concerning its scope and character than with others. (The *ultimate* source of scriptural authority, on nearly any normative account, is God; what is at issue here is the *proximate* source, the link between God and scripture, or — to put it another way — the specific way in which scripture derives its authority from God.) If scripture's authority is essentially a doctrinal authority, a theory of inspiration (plenary or otherwise) might come into play as an account of scripture's authorization as the deposit of divine teaching. Some other accounts of the source of scriptural authority — for example, that it is the record of intense but basically ineffable experiences of divine presence or that it is the human witness to God's mighty acts in history — might be more difficult to reconcile with that view of the scope or character of its authority. A depiction of scriptural authority as having to do primarily with its normative role in shaping faithful dispositions or in providing practical guidance for living might well cohere with an account of scripture's authorization in which scripture is portrayed as an instrument used by God for these purposes. God's present relation to and use of these texts would perhaps be a more prominent feature of such an account than of some others, where the emphasis is on how the texts came to be.

These examples are quite restricted. Their point has not been to provide even a beginning inventory of accounts of scriptural

authority, but rather simply to indicate that to call certain texts
authoritative — and, still more obviously, to follow through by
treating them as authoritative — leads one to a number of decisions
concerning the authority the texts are thought to bear. These decisions affect one's view of these texts in hermeneutically significant
ways. To take a body of texts, such as the Bible, as "scripture"
involves a set of related judgments all of which generally cohere
in an overall synoptic judgment of the texts' character, a basic
construal (to use Kelsey's term) of scripture as a whole. Such a construal is a complex imaginative judgment, as Kelsey has argued.[6]
But though imaginative, it is hardly arbitrary or inexplicable, as
a rule. It is ordinarily informed by certain features of the scriptural texts themselves, by what are taken to be significant aspects
of the interpretive tradition in which the interpreter stands, and by
the interpreter's own sense (however derived) of what normative
Christianity is — that is, of what it is that scripture is supposed
to authorize. None of these three factors — not the intrinsic character of the component texts, the history of their interpretation in
the community, or the interpreter's vision of Christianity — has an
assured priority in the formation of a construal of scripture; the
three are intimately related, and the relative weight of each may
vary from case to case.

In any event, these decisions and the basic construal of scripture in which they cohere have a great deal to do with how one
interprets a given text within scripture *as* scripture. How this is so
might best be indicated by pointing briefly to three closely related
considerations.

It should be clear from these considerations that scriptural authority can mean a number of different things. It would be a
mistake to suppose that the only alternative to the sort of approach
that Delwin Brown or Elisabeth Schüssler Fiorenza advocates is the
rigid and restrictive view of scriptural authority that they themselves use as a foil to their proposals — that is, the view of scripture
as an archetype binding and confining Christians to patterns of
thought and behavior laid down once for all in the past. Certainly this has been a common view — arguably the standard view
throughout most of Christian history — and, as such, it has done
incalculable harm. It deserves the sort of exposure and critique to
which these authors and many others have subjected it. But it represents only one of several possibilities. It ordinarily results from a
basic construal of scripture as a body of divine teachings that are to

be accepted, believed, and obeyed. Prominent as this construal has been historically, there are others that may have far more warrant and that lead in other directions.

In this connection, one of the major values of the recent attention to biblical narrative that the work of Hans Frei has helped to promote is its potential for a reconception of the nature of biblical authority. If a text functions to teach truths that its readers are to believe and to which they are to conform, it will be fairly clear that it means to say that the text authorizes certain beliefs and actions. The text itself sets forth the paradigms. But if a text functions narratively, to disclose a world in which its readers are invited to dwell or to depict a character in relation to whom the readers are asked to see themselves, then the logic of authorization is considerably different. The readers are brought into the narrative; it becomes a context for reflection and action. The insights, convictions, dispositions, and so forth, that the readers achieve in their interaction with the text are, as Brown maintains, the fruits of a struggle. What is achieved is not simply read off the text and accepted but is rather created through the engagement of the readers — who have their distinctive backgrounds and locations — with the text. It is (or may be) authorized by the text, insofar as it is in keeping with the sense of the story. (Not everything that springs from a reader's encounter with a text is thus authorized. The old distinction between what is simply derived from scripture somehow and what is genuinely in accord with scripture has not lost its usefulness.) But what is "in keeping with the sense of the story" cannot be predetermined; it is not latent in the text itself but must be produced through the readers' own engagement with the text. Thus, although the text is normative in that it is by the text that the appropriateness of Christian belief and conduct is to be judged, its normativeness does not stifle diversity and creativity. Indeed, it positively mandates them.

Other basic construals of scripture — for example, a "kerygmatic" construal according to which scripture functions to call forth existential decision — might also be shown to have their own distinctive implications concerning the character of biblical authority, as different from those of the "authorization" model that Brown opposes as are those of a narrative construal. My purpose, however, is not to illustrate or to assess the variety of senses of "authority" and "authorize" that may be associated with various construals of scripture, though the fact that there is such

variety is a point worth reiterating. It is rather to show that the
decisions one makes concerning scriptural authority and the basic
construal of scripture in which they cohere have a great deal to do
with how one interprets a given text within scripture *as* scripture.
How this is so might best be indicated by pointing briefly to three
considerations.

First, a text's status as a component of scripture, under some
definite construal of the latter, may inform an interpreter's judgment as to the sort of text it is — that is, it may inform the
initial decision as to genre that furnishes the reader with a stock
of interpretive procedures and criteria to be applied to the task.

The term "genre" is employed here not in any technical sense
but only to signal the fact that we do have ways of distinguishing among texts and utterances as belonging to different sorts and
of approaching those of each sort with certain expectations concerning how they will work. Writing and speech are ordinarily
governed by conventions, and some of the conventions have to
do with distinctions among sorts of discourse that enable speakers and hearers, or writers and readers, to know how to operate.
Sometimes the conventions dictate that a clear identifying signal be
provided: "Once upon a time..." But even these can be turned
to different uses, and often it is impossible to tell simply from the
form or content of the text or utterance itself to what genre it may
belong. Further, speakers and writers are hardly imprisoned within
established conventions; they are free to modify the given usages,
to adapt literary forms to new purposes, or even to invent new
forms (a move that gives them the task of initiating their audience
into the novelty, if they want to be understood).

The texts of the Christian Bible are of a great many kinds. Many
of the component documents are themselves composed of earlier
texts and oral traditions or of fragments of those. An interpreter
interested in the origins of the traditions found in scripture will
be concerned to find the earliest identifiable genres and, from that
standpoint, might regard their later transformations as corruptions
of an earlier purity. From another standpoint, the same transformations might be regarded more neutrally as transitions to (or the
creation of) new genres, so that a given literary unit might be seen
to belong to several different genres over the course of time. The
historicizing of myth in the formation of Israel's primordial history
and the creation of gospels out of earlier traditions are standard examples of such genre shifts; and interpreters increasingly recognize

the importance of acknowledging them and of asking, for example, what it means to interpret a gospel as a gospel and not simply as a source from which earlier traditions might be recovered. To take that question seriously is not to deny the integrity and importance of the earlier traditions. It is rather to acknowledge that this material may now be read as a new sort of whole and that this task may bring a new set of considerations into play.

To treat a text (such as a gospel) as a component of *scripture* — that is, as a part of a still larger determinate whole — is to take this process one step further. It would be difficult to construe scripture as a whole as belonging to any single genre, and so it is not the absorption of earlier texts into a new genre, or a new single text of a certain genre, that is envisioned here. But certain basic construals of scripture lead one to take its component texts in certain ways — to read them for certain purposes, to identify certain features of them as significant — and this may have an impact on the way one approaches these component texts in their relative independence. The basic construal of scripture that one adopts may suggest specific construals of particular texts within it. It may lead one to apply a certain genre identification to a given text and read it as a text of that sort. It may be that, apart from the scriptural context, some other genre identification would be equally or more fitting; but taking the text *as scripture* opens up the possibility of taking the text, for *this* purpose, according to this construal.

Second, taking a text as a component of scripture furnishes a new context for interpretation. In an essay on the New Testament canon, Harry Y. Gamble observes, "In the nature of the case, canonization entails a recontextualization of the documents incorporated into the canon. They are abstracted both from their generative and traditional settings and redeployed as parts of a new literary whole; henceforth, they are known and read in terms of this collection."[7] The basic construal of scripture with which one operates is likely to affect the resultant "intertextuality," influencing the way in which the texts are read in terms of one another and in terms of the whole that they are taken to constitute. Though the specific implications of such intertextuality will depend upon the basic construal employed, Gamble's claim regarding the New Testament canon is surely applicable to scripture generally: "Since the canon has such results, it cannot be regarded only as an anthology; in its actual effects, the canon is a hermeneutical medium which by its very nature influences the understanding of its contents."[8] From the standpoint of a normative doctrine of scriptural authority, such intertextuality is not simply a historical phenomenon — something that happens to texts when they are assembled into collections under certain conditions — but also a hermeneutical principle.

A third consideration has to do with the principle George Lindbeck has discussed under the name of intratextuality.[9] Whereas "*inter*textuality" designates the way in which a body of scripture serves as an interpretive medium for its component texts, "*intra*textuality" designates the way in which the same body of scripture serves as an interpretive medium for the extratextual world. Rather than interpreting the text in terms of some other, extratextual frame of reference, one asks how the text's own uses of language constitute its distinctive meaning and then uses the text as an instrument through which to interpret the world. As Hans Frei puts it in summarizing Lindbeck, "The direction in the flow of intratextual interpretation is that of absorbing the extratextual universe into the text, rather than the reverse (extratextual) direction."[10] Lindbeck himself articulates the basic understanding of language and meaning underlying this principle in this way: "Meaning is constituted by the uses of a specific language rather than being distinguishable from it. Thus the proper way to determine what 'God' signifies, for example, is by examining how the word operates in a religion and thereby shapes reality and experience rather than by first establishing its propositional or experiential meaning and reinterpreting or reformulating its uses accordingly."[11]

One function of a basic construal of scripture and of the specific understanding of authority that accompanies it is to show how and why this principle of intratextuality is to be followed. The principle itself would seem to be a natural corollary to any adequate doctrine of the authority of scripture, for it simply asserts the hermeneutical priority of scripture over its interpreter. The task of interpretation is to learn the sense of scripture, undertaking whatever development of one's own capacities is requisite to that end, rather than to submit scripture to explanation in terms of one's present knowledge and capacities ("making sense of it") on the assumption that the latter are essentially adequate to whatever scripture may contain.[12] To recognize the authority of scripture is, among other things, to submit one's understanding to it — to be willing to be guided by it and to allow one's previous understandings to be challenged, extended, and transformed by it. Whether this sort of approach is uniquely pertinent to the understanding of *authoritative* texts is, of course, debatable. Lindbeck's judgment (which I share) is that the principle of intratextuality is rooted in more general features of language learning and conceptual growth, so that the procedures would be similar if, say, one were trying seriously to understand a religious faith, or a political perspective, other than one's own. If this is the case, then a doctrine of scriptural authority might serve more as a reminder of good interpretive procedure generally on this point than as an injunction to give these texts special treatment.

The Limits of Scriptural Authority

These three considerations — that a text's scriptural status may properly affect the interpreter's initial judgment as to what sort of text it is; that it provides a context for interpretation; and that it supports the hermeneutical priority of the text — reflect the principal ways in which scriptural status may be taken to be hermeneutically pertinent. It is worth noting, in conclusion, that none of the considerations obliges the interpreter to surrender his or her critical freedom vis-à-vis the text. In the first place, the decision to take a text as scripture and to allow that status and context to affect one's interpretation might well be regarded as a provisional, heuristic decision. It does not prohibit one from also taking the same text in other ways, for other purposes; it represents a desire to investigate what this text, taken as scripture under a certain construal of scripture, might mean. (The necessity of reflecting upon one's concept of scripture and of working out some understanding of the various aspects of its authority as a prelude to interpretation might in fact help an interpreter to avoid letting untested assumptions and attitudes shape the process.)

In the second place, the three considerations in no way oblige the interpreter to accept whatever scriptural texts teach (or disclose, or evoke, or whatever scriptural texts do) as true. Although understanding scriptural texts may require existential engagement, and one may need to grow in certain ways in order to get their point or to inhabit the world they open up, there is still a useful distinction between the logic of discovery and the logic of justification — or otherwise put, between coming to see how things might be, and coming, on reflection, to accept that vision as true. The procedure commended by the principle of intratextuality, or the hermeneutical priority of the text, is then also best understood as a heuristic procedure and not as involving a prior commitment to the truth of what scripture conveys. The point is that one will not be in a position to make an informed judgment concerning the truth of a passage if one does not submit one's understanding, provisionally, to the text.

In the third place, to be guided hermeneutically by the three considerations does not even commit the interpreter to the proposition that what scripture, thus construed, conveys is normatively Christian. One of the ways in which a doctrine of the authority of scripture for the community's life and thought can be tested is by trying it out and discovering what it yields. If it is true that the authority of scripture is not established but rather only acknowledged by the church and that this acknowledgment must be continually renewed, then clearly a doctrine of scripture's authority can play at best only a secondary and instrumental role — principally by suggesting some hermeneutical principles whereby the church's engagement with the scriptural texts might be guided. Whether that engagement leads to a reaffirmation of the texts as the church's scripture or to the deepening of some serious questions over whether they can or should so serve is a question only time and practice may settle.

7

On Being Known

For the word of God is living and active, sharper than any two-edged sword, piercing to the division of soul and spirit, of joints and marrow, and discerning the thoughts and intentions of the heart. And before God no creature is hidden, but all are open and laid bare to the eyes of the one with whom we have to do.

— Hebrews 4:12–13. RSV, alt.

The Book of Hebrews, enigmatic as it is in some respects, contains a number of striking and memorable passages that have been incorporated into the language and self-understanding of Christians. They combine vividness and aptness of expression with a kind of representative capacity, capturing and conveying some common feature of Christian witness and experience with particular vitality. Hebrews 4:12–13 is one such passage. It has a poetic quality; indeed, as with some other passages in the book, some features of language and style indicate that underlying the passage itself is an earlier poetic or hymnic text of unknown origin, a vivid characterization of the word of God that the author of Hebrews has appropriated either directly or in altered form.[1]

The Revised Standard Version translation is essentially uncontested, and I have used it here with minor alteration. Its rendering of the final clause, as "with whom we have to do," felicitously preserves the ambiguity of a cryptic original, which might be "of whom we speak" or "before whom we speak" or (as the NRSV now has it) "to whom we must render an account."

The immediate context of this passage in the Book of Hebrews is one of exhortation and admonition. The author of Hebrews is interpreting Psalms 95:7–11 (RSV: "O that today you would hearken to [God's] voice! Harden not your hearts, as at Meribah") as a word now addressed by the Holy Spirit to those who have heard the message concerning Jesus: Do not harden your hearts against the voice of God, as did that generation whom Moses led out of Egypt, and who, because of their rebellion in the wilderness, were not themselves allowed to enter the promised land. The God who spoke before "in many and various ways" (Heb. 1:1) has now spoken again in Jesus the Christ, offering again the possibility of deliverance — a more complete deliverance (described as "sharing in Christ," that is, sharing the life of his resurrection) than that offered to those whom Moses led. As the deliverance is greater, so also are the potential consequences of its loss through disobedience. And so the author exhorts these new hearers: "Let us therefore strive to enter that rest, that no one fall by the same sort of disobedience. For the word of God is living and active, sharper than any two-edged sword...."

Martin Luther, in his lectures on Hebrews in 1517–1518, took the comparison of the word of God to a two-edged sword as a statement of the horrible punishment that awaits unbelievers: "endless, eternal, and incurable cutting."[2] He rejected interpretations that took these verses to be part of the author's positive exhortation and that understood the word's swordlike work to be that of paring away evil affections and the like — in effect, a cleansing, purifying work. To Luther, it was clear that this passage functions as a warning. It is intended not to reassure us but to terrify us and thus to send us to "that one sanctuary which is Christ."[3]

Luther was surely correct in seeing that, in its context in the argument of Hebrews, this passage has little of comfort about it. It has the force of a warning. But as many modern commentators rightly point out, the intent of the word/sword comparison itself is not to portray the word as an instrument of punishment, but rather to stress its disclosive function. The word finds us out: it penetrates to the innermost parts of our being, discerning the heart. There are no secrets, no hidden things that the word does not reach and open up to "the one with whom we have to do." We cannot hide the truth about ourselves from God, for the word of God will make it evident. It is the fearsomeness of thus being found out — specifically, in the context of Hebrews, of having one's inner resistance to the word, one's "hardness of heart," disclosed — which accounts for the sobering effect of these lines.

But how is this piercing, disclosive character of the word of God to be understood? Words can be disclosive of their speaker, certainly. Sometimes they disclose more than the speaker intends. But here, it is the hearer who is being revealed. Note: the hearer is not being defined or described by the speaker's word — common enough functions of language, of course, for better or worse — but rather disclosed. How might this be?

Sometimes words establish a context for their hearers. This can happen in various ways. If I bring you news of some incident that might have some bearing upon your plans for next week or remind you of some previous commitment you made but forgot, my words obviously do not create the incident or the commitment; they only bring it to your attention. But by doing so, they create a new situation for you. They make a difference, affecting your possibilities for action. Even if you proceed with your plans unaltered, there is an important sense (as a bit of moral reflection upon your action might remind you) in which you will not be doing the same thing. You will have had to take account of what I told you — or to decide to ignore it. In any case, the context for your deciding and acting will have been changed, and your decision and action will have a different character and quality because of my words to you.

There are other cases in which the context-creating function of words is still more striking. Someone who says to you, "I apologize," is not calling your attention to some preexisting fact, but is rather creating a fact, and in doing so is changing the relationship between you. You may accept the apology or refuse it; in either case the situation between you is not the same as it was before the apology. The words of apology have created a new context.

There is a further significant feature to apologies and to a range of similar "speech-acts" (to use the philosopher J. L. Austin's term) that distinguishes them from cases in which the speaker is merely providing some data on the supposition that it might be of interest to the hearer. An apology addresses you personally and calls for a response. Especially if the matter is serious, the quality of your response may reveal a great deal about you. Indeed, being confronted by the apology and by the necessity for coming to terms with it may cause you to learn some new things about yourself. The words addressed to you may travel deep within you and bring you out, so to speak, showing you to yourself and perhaps to others.

Other words addressed to us may have similar and still greater disclosive power in this way. Think of the way in which "I love you," uttered perhaps for the first time in a relationship as a trustful, joyous, yet fearful self-disclosure and self-commitment, can search the hearer's heart. Those words at once establish a new context and call the hearer forth. They permit and also require a response in which, in one way or another, the real character of the hearer is enacted and displayed. Whether the response to such a declaration is honest or evasive, cautious or spontaneous, it is not unusual to feel that it has been a moment of crisis, in the proper sense — a sort of personal audit.

Such examples from ordinary human experience may help to illuminate the notion and the experience of the piercing, disclosive power of the word of God. This word, too, establishes a context, one in which the hearer's innermost reality is called forth. Several of the more abiding ways in which the word of God has been characterized — Hebrew's governing depiction of it as divine promise, for example — point both to its likeness to certain human speech-acts in this regard and to its radical difference. In its address, this word creates the ultimate and inescapable context for its hearers' lives, and in so doing evokes the most profound disclosure of the hearers' selves. Our fellow creatures' words may be mistaken, ill-advised, misleading, or inappropriate; their proper claim on us, however valid, compelling, and important it may be, is always less than ultimate. In responding to one another's apologies, promises, declarations, and so forth, we always have to reckon with our common finitude and fallenness, and try to do the best the situation will allow. But the word of God is always true and fitting, and addresses us in the totality of our being with absolute decisiveness. In its light — as we dispose ourselves in response to it — we are truly disclosed for what we are.

Disclosed to whom? Disclosed, above all, "to the eyes of the one with whom we have to do," who is the speaker of the word. Indeed, the text makes no mention of our being made known to others, nor even of our being brought to self-awareness, by this discerning, sifting activity of this word. The word makes us knowable; but it is God who knows us. The "thoughts and intentions of the heart" may remain hidden, or at best imperfectly disclosed, to human eyes — including the eyes of the one whose heart it is. ("O LORD, thou hast searched me and known me!" says Psalm 139; but also, appropriately, "Such knowledge is too wonderful for me; it is high, I cannot attain it.") It may be, of course, that an encounter with the word of God will lead in a given instance to new self-knowledge, and/or to behavior that makes the truth about oneself more evident to others. But that is a fact of decidedly secondary consequence. What matters ultimately is not our knowledge of ourselves, nor the knowledge of our fellow creatures about us, but our being known by the one God with whom we all finally have to do.

Why, then, is this passage so powerful? It is because it represents a not uncommon experience in connection with what the Christian community has been accustomed to call the word of God, written and preached. That experience may, in fact, have a great deal to do with why we call it the word of God. It is the experience of finding that through this word we are truly known — that the word has brought out the truth about us and that this truth, however dim and fitful our own awareness of it may be, is nevertheless evident to the one whose knowledge finally matters. Luther, in commenting on Galatians 4:9 — a passage that bears comparison in some ways with the one under discussion — sums up its point thus: "Nevertheless, God still knows you."[4] It is not, again, that we have been defined authoritatively, that a picture of ourselves has been imposed upon us from without and that we have been coerced into accepting it. Nor is it that our previous understandings of ourselves have simply been confirmed. It is rather that, in the context created by the word, our own reality has for the first time become manifest.

Apprehending oneself to be thus apprehended is certainly no light thing, as the psalmist knew, and as the author of Hebrews makes clear. "It is a fearful thing," indeed, "to fall into the hands of the living God" (Heb. 10:31). But, given the character of the word that probes us, it can also be the source of a fundamental and exhilarating confidence, and a corresponding freedom. The same writer who calls God "a consuming fire" (Heb. 12:29) can also say, "let us draw near with a true heart in full assurance of faith, with our hearts sprinkled clean.... Let us hold fast the confession of our hope without wavering, for [the one] who promised is faithful" (Heb. 10:22–23).

"Anyone who has ever written sermons," wrote Benjamin Jowett in 1860, "is aware how hard it is to apply Scripture to the wants of his hearers and at the same time to preserve its meaning."[5] The difficulty of which he spoke has probably not diminished substantially in the past century and a quarter. Jowett's own description and treatment of the difficulty in the essay from which I have just quoted still has much to commend it. However, I have quoted his statement not as a prelude to an exposition of his solution, but because it represents a common but, in my judgment, extremely problematic way of stating the problem of interpretation. (I would not, incidentally, want to claim that it represents Jowett's own way of stating the problem. It might be more accurate to say that he is describing the way the problem often appears.) The statement makes it sound as if interpretation is always a particularly unfortunate sort of compromise between the meaning of the text and the wants of the hearers: one's gain is the other's loss. At the extremes, one either renders an interpretation that is faithful to the text but has no relevance to the hearers, or one allows the hearers' wants to determine one's interpretation, thereby losing any semblance of the text's meaning. In the more ordinary, middling case, one produces a mixture of irrelevant faithfulness and faithless relevance.

Against that, I could for the sake of effect almost claim the opposite: it is only when the text is applied to the wants of one's hearers (which may, of course, include oneself) that its meaning can be preserved. But, given the ambiguity of the principal terms, that statement of my thesis would be certain to mislead. It will be better to proceed more circumspectly. There are, I believe, three senses in which the wants of those for whom an interpretation is intended are directly relevant to the interpreter's attempt to render the meaning of the text. I will try to illustrate these with reference to the preceding interpretation of Hebrews 4:12–13.

First, any interpretative effort presupposes an understanding of the aim or aims to be served. The directive "Interpret this text!", apart from any explicit or implicit indication of the purpose of the interpretation, is bewildering. It can only be obeyed if the interpreter assumes (consciously or otherwise) some particular purpose. In this sense, the "wants" of the hearers refers to the hearers' interpretative interest — expressed, implied, or assumed — that the interpreter must determine in order to gain a sense of her or his objectives. This is not to say that the interpreter must take a poll of the intended audience and tabulate the results before proceeding. It is rather to say that the interpreter must make a judgment, on the basis of some understanding of the nature of the hearers' interest in the text, as to the sort of interpretation to be attempted. A close historical exegesis of the tradition embedded in 1 Corinthians 11:23–26 would typically be as out of place as the content of a proper communion sermon as that sermon itself would be on the program of a meeting of the Society of Biblical Literature. The most significant difference between the two instances is not (as is sometimes thought) a difference as to the respective "levels" of the interpretative performance required or of the hearers' capacities, but is rather a difference as to the interpretative interests to be served and of the corresponding interpretative objectives.

Attention to the hearers' wants, in this sense, is indispensable to the task of interpretation. It will not do simply to say that the aim of interpretation is to present the meaning of the text or that it is to enable the hearers to understand the text. What both "meaning" and "understanding" involve depends upon the aims of interpretation in a given case, or sort of case. Nor does it help to stress the word "text" and to say that the aim is to elucidate the text, because there are many cases in which the aims of interpretation are relevant to a determination of what the text is.

An interpreter pursuing a historical interest, for example, might take "Hebrews 4:12–13" to designate that piece of earlier poetic text which the author of Hebrews has incorporated into his or her own treatise and might understand the aim of a historical interpretation to be to explain the circumstances of its origin, the provenance of the terms, images, and ideas, its probable setting and function, and so forth. In that case, the fact that that text is now part of the Book of Hebrews would be relevant only insofar as the text's availability to the author of Hebrews might shed some light upon its earlier history. It is not being interpreted as Hebrews 4:12–13; that is only a convenient way of referring to the text. (Of course, the historian need not be interested only in the earliest form of the text; this is only one possibility.) A student of rhetoric, on the other hand, might be interested in the rhetorical structure and sense of the Book of Hebrews, and "interpreting Hebrews 4:12–13" then might mean giving an account of its literary character, its role within the argument of Hebrews, and so on — questions to which the original setting and sense of the text may be irrelevant. The text is not the isolated passage or its reconstructed *Vorlage,* but rather the passage as a part of the entire document we know as "Hebrews." And a satisfactory interpretation of the text is one that gives an adequate account of it from a rhetorical standpoint. To understand the text (whichever text one has in mind) rhetorically is not the same as to understand the text historically. Different interests are being served, different questions being raised, and different answers sought.

In my own effort in this chapter, I have tried to interpret Hebrews 4:12–13 as Christian scripture. That is, my focus was not on the isolated text or its prehistory, nor simply on the passage as a part of the document known as Hebrews, but rather on the passage as a component of that collection of writings which Christians regard as somehow normative for their self-understanding as Christians and for their understanding of the witness they are commissioned as Christians to bear in the world. My interpretation has been governed by an interest in determining what this text, as Christian scripture, properly contributes to Christians' understanding of themselves and their witness. I have aimed, then, at a theological interpretation — an interpretation that serves critical and constructive reflection upon Christian life and witness as such.

Obviously, this effort has involved some historical and rhetorical considerations. Often some interpretative interests subserve others. It has also involved a particular understanding of the way in that scripture rightly fulfills its authoritative or canonical role — an understanding which is more tacit than explicit in the interpretation itself. Briefly, I believe that different components of canonical scripture — different texts, different genres, different themes — properly serve very different functions in the process by which Christians gain their normative self-understanding from this collection of documents. If that is so, then one question that a theological interpreter must keep in mind while interpreting any scriptural text is the question of the proper canonical function or functions of that particular text.

My own conclusion about Hebrews 4:12–13 in this regard (a conclusion at least partly displayed in the interpretation) is that it has come to be a sort of meta-scriptural comment on the way scripture (among other things) functions as "word of God," namely, by bringing out the truth about our lives and bringing us into a relationship with "the one with whom we have to do" on the basis of that truth. The comment can have various kinds of "perlocutionary" force, to use a term of Austin's once again. By making the comment or by reminding someone of it, one may produce — intentionally or otherwise — any of various effects, depending on the context. It might serve as a warning and be the occasion for repentance: "Righteous as you may appear, there is one who knows the heart." It might, on the other hand, serve as a word of comfort, bringing hope: "Confused as you are, there is one who knows you, and who can finally bring you to yourself." It might — who knows? — even contribute to clarifying someone's understanding of that frequently vexing notion "the authority of scripture."

It is especially in connection with these questions as to how the text might properly contribute to Christian understanding that an interpreter may well learn from the Christian interpretative tradition, including those interpreters who are (sometimes condescendingly) designated as "precritical" — Martin Luther, for example.[6] Granted that there are certain sorts of interpretative interests and issues, especially of a historical character, in connection with which more recent interpreters have a distinct advantage over their predecessors, the older interpreters often have much light to shed upon the bearing of a text upon Christian faith and witness. The fact that a text has been taken a certain way does not, of course, mean that it can or should be taken in the same way here and now. As always, the interpreter must exercise critical judgment over the proposals that come to attention. But the resources of this tradition ought not to be neglected any more than the labors of contemporary biblical scholars ought.

The second sense in which the "wants" of the hearers are pertinent to an interpreter's effort to render the meaning of a text might best be grasped by considering why an interpretation of a text is needed at all. Normally, an interpretation is called for when understanding is somehow problematic: for instance, when the reader or hearer either misunderstands the text, cannot understand it at all, or needs a fuller or more adequate understanding of it. (Any understanding of a text is already an interpretation of it. It is when our natural interpretative activities do not yield the desired result that we speak of "needing an interpretation.") Here, then, the "wants" of the hearers refers to those things that must be supplied if the hearers are to achieve the sort of understanding desired. "Wants" here bears the now archaic sense of *needs* — which may, incidentally, have been part of its sense in Benjamin Jowett's statement.

These "wants" or "needs" may be of different sorts, depending upon the hearers and their situation, and their relation to the text and its situation. At a fairly simple level, information about the text may help — an explanation of the sort of text it is, definitions of terms that are unfamiliar to the hearers, and so forth. Or it may be that some of the concepts used in the text have no place in the lives of the hearers and that these concepts must be taught and acquired if the text is to be understood. Or, possibly, there are factors in the hearers' minds or lives — habits of thought, ingrained attitudes, and the like — that are leading the hearers to misunderstand the text or to be baffled by it. If so, interpreting the text involves identifying these factors and working to overcome their power. Ordinarily, addressing the "wants" of the hearers in some of these respects requires of the interpreter some considerable knowledge of the particular hearers being addressed. That is one reason interpretation must be continually renewed and one reason interpretations do not always travel well. Most of the interpretation of Hebrews 4:12–13 offered above focuses upon another sort of "want," in this second sense, which 1 have (rightly or wrongly) presumed my readers to have, but which at any rate is one that might be widely shared — the "want" of an account that would make the text's principal claim concerning the disclosive power of the word of God intelligible.

My decision to focus upon that presumed need was based in part upon a judgment having to do with the third sense in which the "wants" of the hearers are pertinent to interpretation. Good theological interpretation does not (if I may exploit Jowett's phrasing) *preserve* the meaning of the text, as if in brine; rather, it *activates* it, bringing the text to life and getting it into action. It does so by identifying that point in the hearers' lives at which the text has a use, that question to which it is an answer, that "want" to which it speaks. It is at that point that the text begins to function for what it is.

This is true in principle, *mutatis mutandis,* of any sort of interpretation. In historical interpretation — including that historical interpretation which is normally one component of the theological interpretation of scripture — it has more to do with grasping someone else's use of the text (applying it, so to speak, to the "wants" of its original hearers, if its meaning in that setting is the object of investigation) than with one's own use of it, though the latter is also involved. Presumably, the historian has a use for the text — a reason for undertaking the study of it. Historical interpretation has a point, and historical understanding is demonstrated by the way in which one is able to make appropriate use of the text in the course of whatever one goes on to do with it.

In theological interpretation, concerned as it is with the bearing of the text upon the self-understanding of those for whom it is being interpreted, the "wants" of these contemporary hearers are more directly pertinent. At what point, in connection with what issue or problem, can the text be activated as a means for achieving and sustaining Christian understanding? My own sense of the situation in which a good number of the likely readers of this interpretation find themselves led me to choose Hebrews 4:12–13 as the text for this exercise and then to cast the interpretation as I did in the hope that text and readers might connect.

Our situation, broadly speaking, is one of considerable confusion and conflict over the related issues of authority and rationality in theology and church. There are two opposing tendencies manifest in many treatments and discussions of these issues. They can be designated by some terms once given currency by Paul Tillich. On the one hand, a tendency toward heteronomy is evident in such things as the ever-popular attempts to use formal arguments for the authority of scripture to provide justification for accepting the truth of its content, and in the claim occasionally encountered that Christian truth is *sui generis* and therefore not subject to rational scrutiny. On the other hand, a tendency toward autonomy is sometimes expressed in the rejection of the notion of scriptural authority *tout court* and in the affirmation that nothing in scripture is to be accepted unless it is consonant with the interpreter's own experience and reason. The arguments that embrace each of these tendencies vary a great deal in nature and intention, as does the extent to which the arguments nurture the tendencies. The dangers that the tendencies pose can be brought to mind by recalling Jowett's way of describing the sermon writer's difficulty. In a "heteronomous" approach, the text is exalted and the "wants" of the hearers ignored; in an "autonomous" approach, the "wants" of the hearers are paramount and the integrity of the text is lost.

My own conviction is that the understanding of the character of the word of God that is represented by Hebrews 4:12–13 has much to contribute to an approach to these issues that would avoid these tendencies and their respective dangers. As portrayed by this text — and here this text is rightly representative of the tenor of scripture as a whole — the word of God does not define

reality, heteronomously, imposing a view of self and world that the
hearer is directed to accept. Nor is the word of God something
that simply confirms the hearer's prior attitudes and beliefs. Rather,
the word provides a context within which the truth of things becomes manifest. The promise of this central insight is well worth
exploring.

8

On the Reality of God

In an article in *Religious Studies,* Kai Nielsen continues his examination of the approach to religious belief to which he has earlier given the enduring label of "Wittgensteinian fideism." His specific target is the account of what it means to believe in God offered by the Swansea philosopher Ilham Dilman in various writings, chief among them an article on John Wisdom's philosophy of religion. In Dilman's account, Nielsen finds some features of religious belief helpfully illuminated, especially regarding the connection between believing in God and orienting one's life toward God, a common theme among the Wittgensteinians. At the same time, he finds Dilman not untypically "evasive and in effect obscurantist about how we are to understand the concept of God and about *what* it is we are talking about in speaking of God."[1] Belief in God, on Dilman's account, seems to Nielsen not to differ from taking up a certain moral stance toward the world. How, Nielsen asks, does Dilman's version of Christian believing differ from that of the "Godless Christianity" of Braithwaite, Hare, and Van Buren? Although Dilman seeks to show the sense of God-talk, "he has not been able to articulate a sense of that talk that would distinguish the claims of the believer from those of the religious skeptic."[2]

The problem, as Nielsen sees it, is essentially that of reference. Traditionally, the crucial difference between believers and nonbelievers has been taken to be a disagreement as to what there is: reality either does, or does not, include "a God," and at least some God-talk either rightly or wrongly refers to that God. Dilman wants to excise such references from his account of what believers do and say; and yet, in Nielsen's judgment at least, Dilman does not provide any other satisfactory way of distinguishing believers from nonbelievers, given the fact that nonbelievers may share the moral stance of believers and even use their language, albeit in a deliberately nonreferential way.

It is not my intention to come to the defense of "Wittgensteinian fideism," though it does seem to me that "Wittgensteinian pietism" might be a more apt label, given these philosophers' preoccupation with the religious life, especially its "inwardness" and emotional makeup. Nor do I aim to defend Dilman's position in particular against Nielsen's criticism; I believe that criticism to be warranted and successful on the whole. My purpose is rather to confront the question with which Nielsen's criticism leaves us. How should we distinguish the claims of the believer from those of the skeptic? What should be involved in the believer's affirmation of the reality of God that is not also involved in, say, the "Godless Christian's" recommendation or use of God-language in support of a way of life? "Should" is used in these questions to make it clear that the ensuing inquiry is not simply descriptive — or subtly prescriptive, as some of the Wittgensteinians' accounts of religious believing tend to be — but avowedly normative. This is conceived as a Christian theological response to the question. I say that, not to distinguish it sharply from other responses, but in order to identify the sort of belief (namely, proper Christian belief) that is under discussion here.

Now, it might be supposed that this issue only arises given a somewhat eccentric account, such as Dilman's, of what believing in God amounts to. The first order of business, then, is to show that this is not the case and that, in fact, the question may be fairly provoked by some features of a more standard Christian theological account of God-talk. Nielsen is right in saying that Dilman has called attention to some aspects of our use of God-language that tend to be ignored; and it is some of these aspects, among others, that make the notion of reference problematic.

Dilman notes that believing in God has more to do with having a perspective on the world than with believing in the existence of something within or beyond the world. Believers and nonbelievers need not have different inventories of the world's contents, that is, they can find some basic level at which they are agreed as to what is before them. But they have different ways of relating those contents to each other and to themselves: one will make (or see) connections, have ways of construing things into patterns, that the other will ignore or deny, and vice versa. John Wisdom, in whose work this phenomenon of apprehending relations among things is a recurring theme, is correct in saying that the resultant difference both is and is not a difference "as to the facts," as to what is the case.[3]

Dilman also stresses, in a way that Wisdom does not, the fact that the difference has largely to do with the conceptual equipment of persons, and that coming to believe (or presumably to disbelieve) is often a matter of conceptual growth or change and not a matter of finding new evidence.[4] Whether or not we see a person as loving has to do not only with what we are able to observe about that person but also with our understanding of what love involves; and the more we know about love, the less inclined we are to judge by superficial evidence pro or con. It is this relationship between one's perspective and one's conceptual preparation that lends sense to Wisdom's curious claim that a difference in judgment in such a case both is and is not a difference as to the facts. The evidence may be there for all to see, and, at some stratum of discourse, to agree upon ("She gave him candy"); yet our different ways of "reading" the evidence may yield differing accounts of what is the case, at another level of discourse ("She was expressing her love." "No, she was bribing him."). These different readings display different abilities to make use of the evidence, that is, differing ranges and configurations of concepts for understanding human behavior. And we may modify our reading and come to a different judgment as a result of some shift in conceptuality even when there has been no change in evidence. Thus, one who has long disbelieved in God may one day find belief a possibility, not by finding new data to support the rejected concept, but by discovering that the rejected concept was not an appropriate concept of God. This may lead both to an inquiry after a more adequate concept and to a reconsideration of the evidence, a tentative new reading of the world in the light of a new understanding of what might be meant by "God."

Of course, these are not separate enterprises. If our concepts enable our assessment of the evidence, the evidence also has an impact on our conceptuality. That is, it is through seeing and experiencing samples of love — samples of increasing variety, subtlety, and complexity, and some samples of counterfeit love as well — that we come to understand what love is, and that understanding changes somewhat with each new sample. Our first acquaintance with any such concept comes through examples of its employment, situations in which the relevant terms are used or to which they are somehow applied. We do not normally start out our lives with a definition of love. We may eventually be able to articulate suitable definitions or descriptions for particular purposes, but only after learning our way into the language and behavior of love in a lengthy process of conceptual formation. That this is no less true of the concept of God is another of Dilman's useful observations. "Thus if you wish to understand what God's existence amounts to, ask yourself what it means to believe in God, to worship Him, to thank Him, fear Him, love Him, etc."[5] There is an echo here of Wittgenstein's remark that "grammar tells what *kind* of object anything is."[6] It is by acquainting ourselves with the use of a concept, its "grammar," that we come to see what the concept represents, if indeed it does. "Do we have souls?" is a question that cannot be answered by looking within or around a human body, but only by identifying the contexts in which souls are spoken of, learning the use of the term, and then making a judgment as to whether sense is better served by an affirmative or negative answer. (Sense will be most likely served by an elucidation of the use of the term than by a monosyllabic reply. "There is a soul" amounts to a claim that this concept has a proper application. But simply to make that claim, without suggesting what that application is, is not much help.)

Similarly, the question "Is there a God?" is best approached by way of an examination of the grammar of "God," as Dilman indicates. In what contexts and to what purpose does one speak of God? What does "fearing God," "interceding with God," "praising God" amount to? What is an "act of God" or "the grace of God"? It is through an exploration of such usages in their interrelationships — an exploration that goes beyond verbal acquaintance to conceptual grasp — that one may come to identify God, to see "what it is we are talking about in speaking of God" (to use Nielsen's words).

Nielsen justifiably complains that no such sense of the identity of God emerges from the remarks Dilman makes concerning the proper understanding of God-language. Dilman's practice does not succeed in illustrating his principle that attention to the use of God-language will show us what God's existence amounts to — or if it does, it succeeds only in showing that God's existence doesn't amount to much, since, as Nielsen shows, the reference to God in each of Dilman's examples can be eliminated in translation without any apparent loss in the sense Dilman himself takes them to have. The problem, I believe, is in the practice and not in the principle. Specifically, it is in Dilman's arbitrary restriction of the sense of God-talk to what he considers the "religious" or "theological" sphere, the sphere of inwardness, and his dismissal of other possible dimensions of sense as "metaphysical" or "philosophical." This restriction severely hampers Dilman's ability to deal with the question of the reality of God, in either of the two dimensions of that question. That is, neither the identity nor the actuality of God can be discussed in the terms to which Dilman wants our talk about God to be limited, because those terms exclude some crucial features of "God" even while they permit other features to be highlighted.

Certainly there are metaphysical, philosophical, and even other religious uses of the term "God" that an adherent of a particular religious tradition has every reason to resist, or at least to distinguish sharply from the usage proper to that tradition. There are philosophers' gods that are not the God of Abraham, Isaac, and Jacob. But there is also a sense in which the concept of God native to biblical tradition is a metaphysical concept, after all. Certainly it does not have its origin or its primary *Sitz im Leben* in metaphysical reflection. Like other basic metaphysical concepts, it has its roots and its proper habitat in human experience. It is "metaphysical" only because it has strictly general implications. That is, if it is coherent at all, it is one of those "general ideas" that are, in Whitehead's words, "indispensably relevant to the analysis of everything that happens."[7] It does not take a metaphysician to discern this, nor to admit it. (And admitting it does not commit a person to that "metaphysical religiosity" that Nielsen rightly despises — the use of deep-sounding phrases that only tie the mind in knots when one attempts to understand them.) The affirmation that God is creator of heaven and earth is sufficient, or any of various other biblical utterances stating or implying that God is related to everything there is. It is simply built into the grammar of "God" in this tradition that there is nothing and no event that cannot be described in terms of God's relationship to it — and, indeed, that those who worship God ought so to understand the world, because seeking and operating out of such an understanding is part of what it means to worship God.

Because it is a function of the concept of God thus to structure one's understanding of reality, the question of the reality of God is a strange question. Up to a point, it resembles the question of the reality of love. Imagine someone asking, not "Does she really love him?" but "Is there really such a thing as love?" A pursuit of that question would involve both an effort to clarify what counts as love and an effort to determine whether there are (or have been, or might be) any instances of it. "Love" is a concept that is supposedly applicable to some situations, but not to others, so the question of its identity and that of its actuality are separable in principle. One could fail to find a coherent concept of love, or one could find a coherent concept but fail to find any instances of it.

The question of the reality of God is similarly a question of the coherence and applicability of a concept, except that in this case the second follows from the first. If the concept of God is coherent, there can be no situation to which it does not pertain; coherence entails universal applicability. In this, the question of the reality of God is more like the question of the reality of the world than like that of the reality of love. "If the world isn't real, what is?" is a fair question. Claims that the world is not real usually amount to challenges to our concept of "world" or of "reality" or both. They are not occasioned by such experiences as walking through solid objects or watching furniture disappear, but by the conviction that something else is more properly entitled to the name of "reality." ("And you thought reality meant this. Wait till you see!")

"Reality includes a God" is an odd half-truth. (Wittgenstein is reported to have asked, plaintively, "Couldn't God *half* exist?") The other half is that God includes reality. "God" and "reality" are coextensive, though not identical, concepts. They are coextensive in that there is no reality "outside" or "beyond" God. Whatever there is is immanent in God, so that God is inclusive of all reality. They are not identical concepts, however, because each has uses that the other does not.

The assertion or denial of the reality of God is the assertion or denial of the propriety of a specific way of apprehending and relating to reality. The affirmation of the reality of God does not simply add one more item to the roster of what one takes to be real. Rather, it involves a distinctive way of understanding all that one takes to be real. To be sure, that affirmation also properly implies that God is "a reality." "God" is not simply an honorific term for the world; it has its own distinctive reference, and we can distinguish — though never separate — the world from God. The referentiality of "God" is unusual, however, in that we may refer to God only by referring other things to God, that is, only in language that expressly relates God to other things; while at the same time any statement whatsoever about other things may be understood to permit at least an implicit reference to God. The second of these features is connected with the observation that God is related to everything there is. The first of them is also grounded in the grammar of our talk about God. We may not point to God, except by pointing to something in the world and speaking of God's involvement in it. We may not describe God except in terms of God's relationship to the world. Of course, much of our talk "about" God is not strictly about God at all — that is, it has no direct referentiality or cognitive value — but functions rather to foster a proper human orientation toward God ("The Lord is my shepherd"). But it is an indispensable element of Christian faith, at least, that there is One to whom human beings are relating themselves (or being related) when they use this orienting language. They are assuming not merely a posture, but a relationship. To this extent, at least, belief in God involves referentiality.

"What it is we are talking about in speaking of God," then, is not simply our dispositions, nor simply the world under a different name, but the One who is constitutive of the world as an intelligible whole, related to each of its components, yet distinct from the world thus constituted and determined. What finally distinguishes the position of the believer from that of the religious skeptic is that the believer acknowledges that One, and lives in conscious response to the reality of God — lives, not only as if God were real, but in the belief that God is real.

Whether that distinction is ultimately of much importance, when considered alongside some other significant distinctions among human beings — in the quality and integrity of their lives and of their relationships with others, say — is another question.

9

The Events in Which God Acts

Theological understanding of the notion of an act of God has been notoriously complicated by a common tendency to think of acts of God as extraordinary events. Against this tendency in its popular forms, the young Schleiermacher asserted, "Miracle is simply the religious name for event."[1] And against its more formal elaboration in Protestant orthodoxy, Schleiermacher later advanced his own view of the divine omnipotence, rejecting the distinction between *potentia dei absoluta* and *potentia dei ordinata* and declaring simply that "the entire omnipotence is, undivided and unabbreviated, the omnipotence that does and effects all."[2]

The young Schleiermacher's assertion has had wide currency even among some who would be uneasy with his later theological articulation of its point. But exegetes and theologians attentive to the biblical testimony concerning the particular acts of God have inherited a special problem from the Schleiermacherian settlement. If every event is effected by God, and if no event is especially privileged in this regard, what is to be made of this testimony? One popular solution has been to take the biblical recital of the acts of God as poetic description of certain events that are of extraordinary significance to the reciters and their hearers, though considered as events quite ordinary and explicable. The major question this solution provokes, of course, is: What warrants the selection and interpretation of just these events as especially representative of the divine will? For the biblical witness is surely not simply that these events were important to the identity or survival of the witnessing community, but that God's character and purposes are to be discerned particularly in them, and that it is particularly fitting to recall them as acts of God.

The aim of this chapter is not to survey and assess the variety of proposals that have been or might be offered in response to this question, but briefly to develop one way of regarding the acts of God that may avoid the difficulty from which the question arises. The approach rests upon the crucial, yet far from clear or sharp, distinction between the description of events and the description of acts. Although that distinction has not been foreign to previous discussion of this issue, the two sorts of description overlap so extensively that confusion is never difficult, so some more attention to their differences and relationships may be worthwhile. No attempt will be made ontologically to specify the nature of acts or events, or to distinguish them in definitive terms. Nor will much attention be given to some important distinctions between divine and human acts — differences that would have to be clarified in a fuller account of divine agency. Instead, a few features of our talk about acts and events will be noted and their implications explored with regard to the notion of an act of God.

Acts and Events

As a general rule, the same occurrence may figure in both event-descriptions and act-descriptions: "a notice appeared," "someone posted a notice." It is worth remarking that it is impossible to specify the occurrence common to these two descriptions without indulging in one form of description or the other; that is, either the event (say, the appearance of the notice) or the act (say, the posting of the notice by someone) must be depicted, and there is no reason to suppose that either is closer than the other to the plain unvarnished occurrence, although the context of description may make one more appropriate than the other. Though we can describe an occurrence in different ways, there is no primitive or sophisticated pure description that corresponds to the occurrence-in-itself.

Further, there is no basic form of either event-description or act-description, of which all other event- or act-description is an elaboration. Again, the context of description will ordinarily make one sort more apt than another. In describing my act, it is not necessarily more exact or more truthful to say "I'm making marks on paper" than to say "I'm writing a letter" or "I'm inviting a friend" or "I'm trying to word this correctly." Each of them — even the first, conceivably — could be the most fitting response to "what are you doing?" in a given context, whereas the others might seem more or less devious, odd, or obscure. In describing the same occurrence as an event, similar considerations must determine whether it is more pertinent to depict the event as the making of marks, the invitation to a friend, the struggle for correct wording, or otherwise.

Either sort of description may include the other. The narration of a person's acts may be incident to a description of the events in which they figure, and a portrayal of events may be a part of a rendering of someone's acts, insofar, say, as the acts involve initiating or responding to events that a coherent rendering of the acts must acknowledge as events. At the same time, event-description and act-description may each transcend the other significantly, just as some descriptions in each mode may transcend others in the same mode. The scope of an event-description may be widened to embrace various effects of the focal occurrence within a more comprehensive description of what happened, whereas such a widened scope may be quite inappropriate to a description of the same occurrence as someone's act. Not all the effects of an act are properly regarded as belonging to the act, though they may be included in a description of what happened. At the same time, an act-description may contain features that would be irrelevant to a given event-description involving the same occurrence. (It may be irrelevant to some event-description of my mailing a letter that in doing so I was fulfilling a promise.) The same event, as event, may be ingredient in a great variety of acts, just as the same act may have its place in several different event-descriptions.

The two sorts of descriptions, finally, may not be distinguishable by verbal form. That is, it may not be possible to tell by looking at an utterance which sort of description it is to convey. The terms and locutions of these two efforts are shared to a great extent. A statement such as "the slaves escaped" may be read either way — as a depiction of the slaves' act of escaping, or of the event of the escape (compare "the steam escaped"). "He sat down" may describe a deliberate act or the consequence of a blow to the head. Such ambiguous cases go to show that we must rely on context for an indication of the sort of description being offered. To the extent that it can be discerned whether the description is given in response to an explicit or implicit query of the general form, "What was N. doing?" or of the general form, "What happened?" it should be possible to judge whether act-description or event-description is the more proper reading.

In sum: A particular occurrence may be ingredient in a number of different event-descriptions and act-descriptions, which may overlap in certain respects yet transcend one another in other respects. From this situation two things follow: First, insofar as the various descriptions involving an occurrence overlap, they put some constraints upon one another. Second, insofar as the descriptions transcend one another, it is not possible simply to infer from one description the total range or specific character of other descriptions that might also legitimately be offered. To illustrate these two points: First, if it is correct to say that I mailed a letter, no other valid description of that act (or event) may contradict that one, though other descriptions might take account of it in different ways or perhaps ignore it altogether. And second, it is impossible to read off from that first description the variety of other permissible act- and event-descriptions involving the same occurrence, for example, my fulfilling a promise, breaking the law, or creating a stir at the post office.

God and Events

In the Bible, various occurrences are described as acts of God. Historians may offer a quite different description of these occurrences as events involving human agents and natural phenomena, giving due regard to the thought patterns, beliefs, and interpretative tendencies of those from whom the records of these occurrences derive. It is sometimes alleged that insofar as the occurrences are amenable to ordinary event-description in this way, calling them acts of God is gratuitous or misleading. That allegation can be sustained in one respect: calling an event an act of God may add nothing to our understanding of it as an event. To describe an occurrence as an act of God is not necessarily to claim anything about its character as an event, and a description of the event may very properly take no account of divine agency. But to say that divine agency may be disregarded in a proper description of events is not to say that talk of divine agency has no point or place at all, and this is where the allegation is mistaken. An act of God may be described as an ordinary event; but what is described as an ordinary event may also be an act of God.

Where there is an event, we often infer an act, and with a high degree of success. If a cup of coffee appears on my desk, someone must have put it there. But our inference may sometimes be mistaken, not only in cases of gross mis-description (it was the wind, not an intruder, that rearranged my papers), but also where there is no question as to what happened. You dropped the cup; but was that your act, or was there, say, an involuntary relaxation of your fingers? The occurrence might look the same in either case, down to fine detail. Acts may be ingredient in events, but the act cannot be deduced from the event. Another way to put this is to say that "agency" does not show up in "causation." The fact that *x* is my act does not inevitably betray itself in the sequence of events, no matter how often or how accurately one may connect the events with my action. I do not cause my acts; I simply do them. (If someone asks "How did you move your arm?" I might answer "Like this!" doing it again. I might also be able to supply a physiological account of what caused the arm to move, if that is what the questioner wanted to have. But that would not indicate how I did it.) Neither does God cause God's acts. (This does not mean that something else causes God's acts. The point is grammatical. In this connection it is helpful to remember that the doctrine of creation involves act-description over event-description. There is a world of difference between "what caused the world?" and "who made the world?")

An occurrence's being an act of God, then, will not be evident from a description of the event. But this does not mean that we should posit an act of God in connection with every event, just to be on the safe side. That would be reasonable only on the assumption that God does everything. Although the idea that God is the author of all actions has occasionally been commended as a comfort to believers, it is more commonly regarded as extremely problematic if not unintelligible. It is, in any case, not demanded by the present account. It is one thing to say that God is somehow acting in every occurrence; it is quite another thing to assert that every specifiable event is God's act.

Act and Word

Not only is it impossible to deduce from an event the presence of an act; even given the assurance that an act is involved, the character of the act may still be obscure. Let us say you dropped the cup on purpose; what were you doing dropping it? Were you avoiding burned fingers, expressing your disapproval of the coffee, getting rid of the poison, attracting attention, obliterating the signature on a document by spilling coffee on it...? There are two ways in which we ordinarily learn what an agent's act is. The first is by inference, in which we draw upon our knowledge of the circumstances, of similar incidents, of the agent's previous behavior, and so forth, in interpreting the act. (Often, of course, the inference is so bound up with our very perception of the occurrence that we in effect see the act rather than first seeing an occurrence and then supplying an interpretation. It is only incidents of mistaking what we see that alert us to the inferential character of the process.) The second way is through the agent's own account of the act — a disclosure of intention, perhaps, or a reply to the query "What were you doing just then?" Neither of these routes to an understanding of an act is absolutely reliable. We may be mistaken in our perception or interpretation, and the agent may be confused, untruthful, or self-deceived. Nevertheless, this is how we come by our understanding of the acts we witness or suffer.

Our awareness of the acts of God must travel one of the same routes as our awareness of other agents' acts. Only in this case a certain primacy must be given to disclosure over inference. Any capacity to infer (or to perceive) a human act in connection with an occurrence is necessarily grounded in some previous acquaintance with the typical features of similar acts or the behavior of similar agents, that is, other human beings. But in God we have to do with an agent who is in crucial respects unique and whose acts are strictly unpredictable. That there is a God who acts at all is not something a careful observer of the world's occurrences is inescapably driven to conclude. And even assuming that there might be, any transition from that assumption to an account of where and how God is acting is fraught with difficulties, to say the least. Indeed, it is a risky business to try to infer from a knowledge of God's previous acts what God's current and future acts may be. This is why any attempt to state very specifically "what God is doing in history" as a reference point for one's own actions is exceedingly problematic. The problem is not that God acts whimsically. God is the most constant and consistent of agents. The unpredictability roots rather in our inability to specify the particular ways in which God's steadfast purposing may be being enacted under given circumstances. Not only is our own reading of events *sub specie aeternitatis* far from disinterested, it is, simply, not God's. (God is faithful; but the people of God have found that that faithfulness may be exercised in acts similar to, or quite different from, what has gone before. This has been a hard lesson, and it is one still commonly resisted.)

It is therefore from God that we first learn of the acts of God. That is, it is the word of God that identifies and interprets to us the acts of God, which are otherwise undiscernible in events. This priority of "word" over "event" in our coming to apprehend the acts of God must be respected in any adequate account of God's self-revelation. God is not "revealed in history," if history is understood as the course of events. God does indeed act in events, as our title suggests, but the events as such do not betray that fact. We do not arrive at a knowledge of God by noticing the Godly features of certain events and following God's footprints through history, so to speak. Even "God is revealed in acts" is an abbreviated and therefore potentially misleading statement of the order of knowing involved. The acts of God themselves must be disclosed as God's acts. God is hidden in events and is revealed as acting only through the word that renders the acts as God's acts to us.

Of course, that word is also hidden to the undiscerning eye or ear. The word of God, like a human word, is mediated through occurrences. The act by which a word is performed, by voice, pen, gesture, or whatever means, is an occurrence that could also be studied and described as "event," for example, in terms of physiology or physics. God's word is God's act; but its occurrence may also be readily amenable to description as a human word or act, or as an event among other natural phenomena. God speaks where and when God wills. The hearing of that word is likewise an occurrence subject to a variety of depictions. But however the apprehension of the divine word happens and however else that happening may be described, theologically it is to be understood as a hearing enabled by the grace of God in that coincidence of word and Spirit which marks God's self-actualizing self-disclosure.

"The Word, the Word, the Word," wrote Luther, " ... even if Christ were given for us and crucified a thousand times, it would all be in vain if the Word of God were absent and were not distributed and given to me with the bidding, this is for you, take what is yours."[3] The context of this remark was a discussion of the Lord's Supper, but the point is applicable to the broader issue. God's action in the sacraments, like God's action in other occurrences, must be disclosed and made appropriable through the word. According to Augustine's widely accepted understanding, a sacrament comes to be when the word is engaged with an element ("Accedit verbum ad elementum et fit sacramentum").[4] In the sacrament, God's gracious action (traditionally — and somewhat problematically — the *res*) is both accomplished and manifested through the sign-act (the *signum*), the "visible word" that unites word and element. Without the word, there is no sacrament; without the word, there is no manifestation of the acts of God.

Thus, to describe an occurrence as an act of God is not to indulge in a pious overdescription of the events involved, justified perhaps by their impressiveness. It is instead to place the occurrence within a different context of description, on the basis of the agent's own self-disclosure. It is to acknowledge a God who not only acts, but also speaks.

10

The Aim of Christian Theology

"Divinity is nothing but a grammar of the language of the Holy Ghost." John Wesley cites this remark of Luther with approval in the Preface to his *Explanatory Notes Upon the New Testament.*[1] To a modern reader, the remark may sound more quaint than apt. It would not be likely to bring much clarity about theology to the uninitiated, though it might bewilder them further. Neither theologians nor nontheologians would find it very helpful if it were pressed into service as a straightforward definition of theology. It is clearly a metaphor, capturing and expressing quickly a certain understanding of theology. But as a metaphor, it may still be provocative, even if not immediately enlightening. In part, it is even topical: the notion of "theology as grammar" has received some attention in recent years as a result of Ludwig Wittgenstein's single parenthetical use of that phrase in a passage in his *Philosophical Investigations.*[2] Perhaps it is time for another look at Luther's remark. Could it possibly serve as a useful characterization of the theological task in our own time? I believe it might, if we can overcome its initial strangeness enough to explore its implications.

Spirit, Scripture, and Language

Recovering its force may not be easy. "Theology as grammar" may have a future or at least a present. But "the language of the Holy Ghost" — ? The phrase may evoke memories of a biblicism now for the most part mercifully abandoned, in which scripture was seen as the product of divine dictation, the Spirit's own words recorded by human amanuenses. If this is what the phrase means in Luther's epigram — if it is only a loaded circumlocution for "scripture" — then it is better left forgotten. But surely that would be a misunderstanding. A refusal simply to equate scripture with "the language of the Holy Ghost" is not only proper but vital, and the failure of Protestant Orthodoxy several centuries ago to maintain their distinction had tragic and far-reaching consequences.

The language of the Holy Spirit is not to be identified with scripture any more than that much more familiar concept, the word of God, is to be identified with scripture. There are at least three reasons to resist such identification. First, and obviously, the Bible is not a language. It is written in language (or languages), but it does not constitute a language in itself. Language involves far more than any single document or collection of documents. A language is more than its utterances.

The second reason may sound just as obvious, but its consequences will require a somewhat longer treatment. It is that the language of the Bible is definitely human language. This claim has not, in fact, always seemed so commonplace. One may still hear occasional praise of biblical language and style (especially in the King James Version) as *sui generis,* heavenly, beyond human attainment. Johann Salomo Semler's salutary and commonsensical objection to Protestant Orthodoxy's characterization of scripture as "divine language" has not outlived its usefulness, though it dates from 1783: "But surely there is no 'language of God' or 'language of the Holy Spirit.' Language belongs to human beings."[3] The discovery over a century later that the language of the New Testament was not a special dialect but simply the common (*koine*) language of its environment reinforced Semler's observation. The language of scripture is for the most part not only human language, but vernacular language at that.

What then is the relationship between scripture and whatever is meant by "the language of the Holy Spirit"? Semler's own solution — and he has had much company — was to say that although scripture *is* not the word of God, it *contains* the word of God. The Spirit "speaks," somehow, within or behind the human language of the text. Interpretation, in this view, is a refining process in which the meaning of the text is separated from the vehicle in which it is found. The Word must be freed from the words. The further this hermeneutical model is pursued, however, the more tenuous the relationship between language and meaning becomes. It is not difficult to see why this is so. In our ordinary use of language we are familiar with the conventional twists by which more meaning, or a different meaning, may be sprung from an expression than its obvious sense would allow. (Such figures of speech were indeed once commonly called "tropes," i.e., "turns.") Because we are acquainted with such ways of taking liberties with literal meaning, they generally enhance and enliven communication rather than blocking it. We may be momentarily bewildered by new expressions, but we soon assimilate them, so that a surprising proportion of our vocabulary consists of petrified metaphor. Our ability to understand and enjoy odd uses of words is contingent upon our observance of fairly stable and dependable conventions in most of our speaking, through which meaning is connected with verbal sense. That is, most of the time, people mean what they say; and it is this which enables us to recognize a figure of speech as such when we encounter it. Now if this connection between meaning and verbal sense is severed at the outset, on principle, in an interpretative effort — if we see language as a cloak that may as readily obscure as protect meaning or as a husk that must be peeled away from meaning and discarded — it is only natural then for "meaning" to come to be described in nonlinguistic terms and for words to be increasingly distrusted and disvalued. When this view of the relationship between language and meaning prevails, not only that odd phrase "the language of the Holy Spirit," but even that more common and central term "the word of God" seems less and less useful, as meaning is depicted perhaps as "experience" or "event."

But there is another way of grasping the relationship that may hold more promise. Rather than saying either that scripture *is* the word of God or that it *contains* the word of God, we may say that scripture is *potentially* the word of God; it may become the word of God under certain circumstances. This dynamic view of the relationship between text and Word is certainly no novelty. It is consistent with Luther's own understanding of the relationship between letter and Spirit, and recurs here and there in more recent theology. For Karl Barth, for instance, revelation takes place "when and where the biblical word becomes God's Word, that is, when and where the biblical word comes into play as a word of witness."[4] Ernst Käsemann affirms that scripture "can only become the word of God so long as we do not seek to imprison God within it," but that it can also become "the letter," with destructive results, when it is separated from the Spirit.[5] Here, emphatically, the Word is not "contained" by the words; the words may, or may not, become the Word.

Put in terms of our metaphor, the language of scripture may become the language of the Holy Spirit. When? When it functions as such in the lives of its readers or hearers; when, perhaps, it grants them a new apprehension of the ultimate context of their lives, or new attitudes, or new concepts, or sustains and strengthens those previously granted — when it opens to them the life of faith, hope, and love, and nourishes them in that life. Augustine and Luther are among a rather large company who could testify to the sudden illuminating power of a passage of scripture as it came alive at a critical point for them. In perhaps less dramatic but no less important ways, scriptural perspectives, themes, and concepts inform the lives of all Christians. To the extent that scripture thus enables life "in the Spirit," it becomes the language of the Spirit.

But certainly scripture is not the only material that can function in those ways. And that leads at last to the third reason for resisting any identification of the language of the Spirit with scripture: scripture represents only a sample of that language. It is found more commonly outside the canon of scripture, in the living language of the community of faith — in preaching ("the word of God proclaimed," in Karl Barth's usage), the liturgy (where "the Spirit speaks again," in Yves Congar's popular phrase), hymnody, the language of prayer and devotion, of teaching, of conversation. The language of faith in all of its forms and uses is potentially the language of the Holy Spirit. And the possibility should not be excluded that uses of language other than the explicitly "faithful" may also have this potential. Secular language need not be domesticated to Christian uses to function in this way. Secular literature and the literature of other religious traditions may become the word of God for a particular reader or listener, entirely apart from any Christian mediation or gloss. This much may be affirmed in principle by anyone who does not want to confine the Holy Spirit within the church. The language of the Holy Spirit need not always adopt a conventional Christian vocabulary, nor appear under Christian auspices, any more than it must restrict itself to the bounds of scripture.

Scripture is not the exclusive locus for the word of God, then;

but it has traditionally been regarded as the canon or standard of judgment for those who deliberately seek to use language effectively in the service of faith, that is, to use language in such a way that it might become the Spirit's language. Scripture is the canon because it not only can become the word of God like other literature, but actually has become the word of God in a great variety of circumstances. Its potential has been realized anew with great reliability, yet at the same time with a challenging and often revolutionary impact. The community of faith, remembering the power of this material to re-present the Word afresh to each new situation, believes that it will always have to account for its own use of language and its own stewardship of life in the light of this in-breaking Word from scripture. That is a far cry from proof-texting one's assertions with quotations from the Bible, as if the word of God were already set in the words of the text as in concrete, and hearing and understanding were finished.

There is some significance in the fact that our canon is an unruly lot of material, which resists systematizing, reduction to essentials, or even harmonization. The Christian canon is not a creed, formula, or definition of the "essence of Christianity" from which all correct doctrine and action might be inferred. Instead, it is a whole rambling collection of diverse utterances spanning several centuries, cultures, and conceptualities, embracing many literary genres and techniques. Taken comprehensively, it functions less as a limitation than as a goad to our own thought. The canon challenges its users to become more flexible, more sensitive to the abundant variety of possibilities for embodying Christian witness. (A good lectionary draws our attention to the diversity of the canon in just this way, urging us to bring the whole canon to bear appropriately upon our thought and life.) We have not yet exhausted the possibilities suggested by the canon of scripture, and those who work with it in any depth generally discover it to be a stimulus rather than a limitation to creative reflection and expression.

Again, this is not to suggest that all that we say must be derived from scripture. Canon does not mean source, and even though scripture may in fact always remain the primary source of our thought, its function as canon is not to supply all our ideas but to enable us to judge their adequacy, their likelihood of usefulness within the language and life of faith. Of course, the canon cannot properly function as canon in any mechanistic way but only when it has itself become a living text, informed by the Spirit. The norm for both interpretation and witness is never finally in our possession. Meanwhile, insofar as Christians understand themselves to be the historically formed covenant people of God, whose charter and text is that collection of documents known as the Old and New Covenants, scripture will always be more than either a source of ideas or a canon of critical reflection, as it functions in numerous ways to nurture and shape the life and language of that people.

Theology as Grammar

Human language is potentially the language of the Holy Spirit. The language of faith, or of the Christian community, is the language of people who bear that possibility in mind and who use their language in the hope that it may also be used by God. Now, what does it mean to speak of theology as the grammar of that language in which the Spirit speaks?

In a broad, basic, and nontechnical sense, grammar is that sort of reflection on language which reveals how words and larger expressions are to be taken, in their various uses. It was in this broad sense that Wittgenstein employed the term. (He never defined it more exactly than to say he was using the term "in its ordinary sense," as "any explanation of the use of language."[6]) Grammar shows us what place we assign to a word in a given construction and situation; it "tells what *kind* of object anything is."[7] For instance, to note that "red" designates a color in one sentence, a person in another, and a warning in a third is to note some features of the grammar of those three expressions. Grammar is not concerned with words and expressions "in themselves," in isolation from contexts, for their grammar can only be discerned in their use. "How words are understood is not told by words alone," Wittgenstein observed — and then he added "(theology)."[8] Adducing theology in that instance might have seemed highly appropriate to Luther. For all his insistence on searching out the plain grammatical sense of scripture and avoiding flights of exegetical virtuosity — an insistence that was not just empty talk — Luther also was ready to claim that "the Holy Spirit has his own grammar," and that, for example, no one can speak of the Trinity who is not ready to adopt some new grammatical principles.[9]

Theology as grammar, then, tells us how to take the language of faith. It discloses its sense. It is an aid to those who would speak and understand that language, helping them to avoid mistakes and misapprehensions so that they can get along with the language. It is especially helpful, it may be supposed, where the requirements of faithful speaking put some strain on ordinary grammar, as in Luther's example, or where apparent similarities to other sorts of language may mislead the hearer, or where a new context or a new challenge calls for new developments in the language. Does the Christian doctrine of creation imply a hypothesis concerning the origin of species? How may the concepts of sin and salvation be related to psychological understandings of the human condition and human potential? What is the bearing of Christian hope upon social and political struggle?

It is the task of theology as grammar to discern the various uses to which language is put in the service of Christian witness. It distinguishes among the sorts of claims being advanced at different points, as well as ascertaining what claims are not being made. It points out what implications might properly be drawn from the central affirmations of that witness and what implications are best avoided. It determines the relative weight or force of the various themes and affirmations so that what is properly central may be identified. It attempts to distinguish assertions from assumptions — that is, what is being said, or the "point" of an utterance, from the framework of assumptions (which may or may not be actually germane or binding) within which it is said. It attempts to distinguish the local and temporary elements of a previous statement from what is of more general validity in it — not in order to produce an eternally valid abstraction, but so that the statement may address a new situation with full attention to that situation's own particularity. Theology tries to secure to each part and facet of the language its own integrity and rightful power.

Most people don't begin to learn a language, either their native tongue or another, by studying books of grammar, but by picking up phrases and expressions and becoming acquainted with their use, gradually increasing their mastery. And most people don't learn the language of faith by studying theology. People have recourse to theology, as to grammar, when they become aware of some difficulty in their understanding and use of the language or when they want to gain proficiency of a certain kind. One might properly turn to theology to resolve a confusion about the meaning of faith or to enhance one's understanding of human behavior.

One might bring theological resources to bear upon the question of one's political responsibility in a given situation. More generally, some theological ability is a necessity for those who venture to lead or to represent the church, and that ultimately means for every Christian in that every Christian may be called upon to bear witness under circumstances demanding an informed and creative response. Theological study may be useful here for improving one's abilities. Of course, not all the problems people have with Christianity or with themselves are theological, and it may be a mistake — though perhaps also a sign of our exceeding confidence in technology — to seek a theological solution to a problem that in another perspective might be recognized as a spiritual or moral one. Nor does proficiency in the Christian life require a theological education. The values of theology, though many and important, are not all-encompassing.

Theology as grammar helps us to use a language. Being helped in a language is something different from being offered a translation. A grammar is not a translation. It does not tell us in other words what the original language means. It is not a second language, superseding the primary idiom, but, simply, a guide to the use of that primary idiom. Theology has sometimes been understood as a new language, and theologians have occasionally tried to demonstrate the adequacy of their theological model by translating as much of the language of faith as they could into the new parlance. But "theology as translation" seems cumbersome at best: by focusing on the material problems involved with finding or devising a new idiom into which the meaning of the old could be transposed, it limits its own usefulness, meanwhile fostering the notion that the aim of theology is to produce a new vocabulary and conceptuality, a new home for Christian meaning.

But theology understood as grammar is released from this pressure to restate everything. A grammar is not the language itself, nor a reconceptualizing of its concepts. It is not the aim of grammar to say everything there is to say, but to discover to us the workings of the language so that we may continue to use it properly. The aim of theology as grammar is not to render the primary language of faith obsolete, but rather the opposite — to insure its continuing accessibility and vitality. An understanding of the grammar, acquired through study or simply in use, enables us to use the natural language without stumbling, without self-consciousness, and without mental reservations — to be at home in it.

Critical and Constructive Dimensions

It begins to sound as if "theology as grammar" is, whether subtly or overtly, unconsciously or deliberately, a servant of the status
quo. If the task of theology is only to describe the use of the language of faith, does it thereby abandon any critical or constructive
role and merely describe prevailing convention? Luther's metaphor
might be read this way, as an injunction against theological pre-
sumptuousness: who are we to tamper with the language of the
Holy Ghost? Properly humbled by that reminder, we could sit
down to trace and reproduce the patterns of the past, as preserved
definitively in Holy Writ. To give the metaphor this conventional-
ist application, however, would be already to erase that important
distinction between the language of the Holy Spirit and our own
language, including scripture. We have already seen that their relationship is not one of identity but of interesting tension and
potentiality. Theology deepens our understanding of that dynamic
relationship, increasing our awareness of both the insufficiency and
the promise of our language. Grammar may not be so innocent and
innocuous a study after all. Rather than leaving us content with the
present state of our language, it is likely to make us less satisfied.
Recalling how easily words that were "Spirit" may become "letter," we may recognize the oppressive potential of what is intended
as a liberating message. Knowing how readily words may be mis-
construed, we may be less inclined merely to repeat ourselves, more
willing to engage in the continual critical reshaping of our speech.

Wittgenstein remarked that "the aim of the grammar is nothing but that of the language."[10] That remark indicates precisely
the aim of theology understood as grammar. Its aim is to show
how the language of faith may best fulfill its own aim, which is
to serve as the language of the Holy Spirit, the language in which
God addresses us. It allows us to judge, with all due trepidation,
the extent to which the language of our past and present may have
furthered or hindered its own authentic aim. That is, it permits the
criticism of tradition and of current practice. At the same time, a
grasp of the grammar enables one to participate responsibly in the
extension, reformulation, and general growth of the language of
the community that seeks to bear witness to God. Though it may
be inappropriate, on this understanding, to think of theology itself
as translation, the growth of the language of Christian faith has often involved the translation or reconception of basic themes out of

older levels of the language in order to meet new situations. Even if theology were to renounce any innovative role, as outside its proper scope, it would still have the task of monitoring this process of growth. In fact, however, theologians themselves have generally been experimenters and innovators whose suggestions have occasionally been influential for a shorter or longer period in the thought and language of the church. Theology can lead to the enrichment of the language and to a critical and creative rather than an unthinking appropriation of the tradition.

Of course, it is precisely a familiarity with the historical and conventional language of the community, an immersion in it, that allows one to adapt it freely — like a native speaker who is able to respond sensitively and openly to the needs of a new context, rather than like a tourist who is limited to repeating phrases out of a guidebook. One who is at home in the language may take surprising liberties with it. It is when the language is our own that we can change it. We make it our own just by exercising that ability to shape it to current needs. It is when, for instance, we take the Bible as our own text, as a literature in our own language, that its story can be retold in our own words. That happens most readily when we do not approach the Bible only as an alien document, the record of an ancient people, and try to make sense of it, but when we instead set ourselves to learn the sense it has and to become critical participants (in actuality or in spirit) in the community whose life and witness is first recorded there.

If this should raise the specter of a dogmatic prohibition of or interference in the critical investigation of scripture, then it is time to invoke J. S. Semler again, as the representative of those who rightly insist that historical-critical study should be free from guidance by dogmatic interests or presuppositions. This claim can be granted all the more readily, however, and the positive results of such free critical inquiry for theology acknowledged and received, when we recognize that it does not mean that the canon of scripture as presently constituted is of no direct theological usefulness or that a critical historical reading of scripture is the only valid sort of reading. Critical historical inquiry discloses earlier forms and stages of the witness of the community of faith, the settings within which that witness was formed and expressed, and the transformations the language of faith has undergone in its early history. Such knowledge is valuable both to our understanding of the biblical writings in their present shape and to our reflection on the possibilities of Christian witness in our own time. Theology may benefit greatly from this study without its obviating a careful appreciation of the interpretation and use of scripture before — and again beyond — critical historical investigation. We can claim all the forms and transmutations of the language of faith as our own linguistic heritage. It is an amazingly complex and convoluted linguistic heritage. But it is well to try to come to terms with it as it stands, rather than enforcing an alien order or simplicity upon it, for — to some extent at least — its complexity answers to the complexity of human life itself.

"Divinity is nothing but a grammar of the language of the Holy Ghost." The force of Luther's metaphor may be appreciated even by those who would not be ready to concede that theology is "nothing but" such a grammar. In our time, at least, it would seem that theology must be a great many things precisely in order for it to be an effective grammar. It would be unwarranted to read the metaphor as an invitation to abandon the various theological disciplines and their methods or to sever the relationships between theological and cognate disciplines and seek some primitive austerity and purity. A map of the theological enterprise must be sought elsewhere. Luther's metaphor does not tell us how theology is to be organized or even by what methods it is to proceed. It only reminds us what theology is for. And that is not a gratuitous reminder, but one that seems continually appropriate.

Notes

1: An Invitation to Theological Study

1. Daniel W. Hardy and David F. Ford, *Praising and Knowing God* (Philadelphia: Westminster Press, 1984), p. 71.

2. For some development of the view of theology sketched here, see Charles M. Wood, *Vision and Discernment: An Orientation in Theological Study* (Atlanta: Scholars Press, 1985).

3. George Burman Foster, "The Contribution of Critical Scholarship to Ministerial Efficiency," *American Journal of Theology* 20 (1916): 178.

2: Theological Education and Education for Church Leadership

1. David B. Burrell, *Aquinas: God and Action* (Notre Dame, Ind.: University of Notre Dame Press, 1979), p. 4.

2. I do not mean to imply that only Christians can understand the Christian faith. However, an understanding of the Christian faith — or of any other religious tradition — does seem to require a kind of conceptual equipment that is normally achieved through personal participation in it. The task confronting the person who wants to understand a faith other than her own is to "entertain" that faith sufficiently to acquire the relevant concepts, through whatever sort of involvement is both necessary and appropriate. This is less difficult in some cases than in others, for a variety of reasons, but it is probably never easy.

3. There are other forms of theology and of theological education than Christian. To what extent, if at all, what I say about the Christian versions would be true of other traditions (for example, Jewish theology and theological education) is best left to members of those other traditions to judge. For more on the general understanding of Christian theology and theological education represented here, see Charles M. Wood, *Vision and Discernment: An Orientation in Theological Study* (Atlanta: Scholars Press, 1985).

4. Regarding the moral aspect of Christian witness (its injunctions, recommendations, and so on, concerning human conduct), one might substitute "right" for "true" in the second category — depending on how one construes the logic of moral claims. There is a highly illuminating treatment of the possible relations between claims to authenticity and truth or rightness in religious traditions in William A. Christian, Sr., *Doctrines of Religious Communities: A Philosophical Study* (New Haven: Yale University Press, 1987).

5. I am indebted to my colleague Professor Joseph L. Allen for his reflections on this theme in a convocation address at Perkins School of Theology.

6. Rudolf Bultmann's critique of what he called "pious theology" in his introductory lectures on theological study makes this point very well, as has Schubert M. Ogden in various places. See Rudolf Bultmann, *Theologische Enzyklopädie,* ed. Eberhard Jüngel and Klaus W. Müller (Tübingen: J. C. B. Mohr [Paul Siebeck], 1984), pp. 163–67; and Schubert M. Ogden, "Christian Theology and Theological Education," in *The Education of the Practical Theologian,* ed. Don Browning et al. (Atlanta: Scholars Press, 1989), pp. 21–35.

7. See Wood, *Vision and Discernment,* pp. 46–49, 95.

8. Thomas C. Oden's *Pastoral Theology: Essentials of Ministry* (San Francisco: Harper & Row, 1983), exemplifies both of these problematic features. Pastoral theology is concerned with "the systematic definition of the pastoral office and its function" (p. x), and "shepherding" is the "pivotal analogy" (pp. 49–63). Because these are matters of deliberate decision for Oden, his book provides a good contemporary indication of what is gained and lost thereby.

3: "Spiritual Formation" and "Theological Education"

1. George A. Lindbeck develops this point (following the lead of Robert Bellah et al. in *Habits of the Heart*) in his very useful article "Spiritual Formation and Theological Education," *Theological Education* 24 (1988), Suppl. 1: 15–16. The subject of the spiritual state of students in a number of theological schools has received more widespread attention through Paul Wilkes's article "The Hands That Would Shape Our Souls," in the December 1990 issue of *The Atlantic Monthly.*

2. Lindbeck, "Spiritual Formation and Theological Education," p. 12.

3. Werner Krusche, "Geistliche Begleitung im Theologiestudium," in *Kirchlicher Dienst und theologische Ausbildung,* ed. Helmut Begeman and Carl Heinz Ratschow (Bielefeld: Luther Verlag, 1985), p. 218. As the title indicates, Krusche prefers "spiritual guidance" to "spiritual formation" as a name for this aspect of theological training.

4. Although I will be discussing church leadership in its typical forms

here, the general points should apply *mutatis mutandis* to religious leadership (and education for it) in some other traditions.

5. Michael Walzer, *Interpretation and Social Criticism* (Cambridge: Harvard University Press, 1987), p. 61.

6. In *To Understand God Truly: What's Theological About a Theological School* (Louisville: Westminster/John Knox Press, 1992), David H. Kelsey stresses the importance of moving beyond thinking of "theological education" in the abstract to considering "the theological school" as its concrete embodiment, and also identifies some of the key factors that might help us understand the distinctive identity of a particular school. I am indebted to him on both counts.

4: The Knowledge Born of Obedience

1. John Calvin, *Institutes of the Christian Religion,* trans. Ford Lewis Battles, Library of Christian Classics, vol. 20 (Philadelphia: Westminster Press, 1960), I, 6, 2, p. 72.

2. See Karl Barth, *Church Dogmatics,* I/1, trans. G. W. Bromiley (Edinburgh: T. & T. Clark, 1975), p. 18, where Calvin's dictum is cited. On the principle among liberation theologians, see José Míguez Bonino, *Doing Theology in a Revolutionary Situation* (Philadelphia: Fortress Press, 1975), ch. 5, and the literature cited there; also James Cone, *God of the Oppressed* (New York: Seabury Press, 1975).

3. Immanuel Kant, "What Is Enlightenment?" in *The Philosophy of Kant,* trans. and ed. Carl J. Friedrich (New York: Modern Library, 1949), p. 132.

4. Blaise Pascal, *Pensées,* trans. A. J. Krailsheimer (New York: Penguin Books, 1966), pp. 149–53. Peter Boehler's remark is cited in *John Wesley,* ed. Albert C. Outler (New York: Oxford University Press, 1964), p. 17.

5. Martin Luther, "Preface to the Epistle of St. Paul to the Romans," trans. Charles M. Jacobs, in *Luther's Works,* vol. 35, ed. E. Theodore Bachmann (Philadelphia: Muhlenberg Press, 1960), p. 378.

6. Ludwig Wittgenstein, *Remarks on the Foundations of Mathematics,* trans. G. E. M. Anscombe (Oxford: Basil Blackwell, 1964), p. 29.

7. Pascal, *Pensées,* pp. 39–40.

8. Here I am following Michael Foster's helpful, brief characterization of the conversion of the intellect in his *Mystery and Philosophy* (London: SCM Press, 1957), pp. 46–47.

9. Ludwig Wittgenstein, *Philosophical Investigations,* trans. G. E. M. Anscombe, ed. G. E. M. Anscombe and Rush Rhees (3d ed.; New York: Macmillan Co., 1958), sec. 400.

10. Jonathan Edwards, *Religious Affections,* ed. John E. Smith (New Haven: Yale University Press, 1959), pp. 272–73. John Wesley, "An

Earnest Appeal to Men of Reason and Religion (1743)," in *The Works of John Wesley,* vol. 11, ed. Gerald R. Cragg (Oxford: Clarendon Press, 1975), pp. 46–47.

11. See John Wisdom, "Gods," in his *Philosophy and Psycho-Analysis* (Oxford: Basil Blackwell, 1969).

12. Bernard Lonergan, S.J., *Method in Theology* (New York: Herder & Herder, 1972), p. 238.

5: Finding the Life of a Text

1. Hans W. Frei, *The Eclipse of Biblical Narrative: A Study in Eighteenth and Nineteenth Century Hermeneutics* (New Haven: Yale University Press, 1974), pp. 96–104.

2. Christian Wolff, *Vernünftige Gedanken über den Kräften des menschlichen Verstandes und ihren richtigen Gebrauche in Erkenntnis der Wahrheit,* ed. Hans Werner Arndt, *Gesammelte Werke,* I:1 (Hildesheim: Georg Olms, 1965), pp. 140–41.

3. Credit for giving this distinction its place in modern theology is given to the Wolffian theologian Sigmund Jakob Baumgarten by Emanuel Hirsch, *Geschichte der neueren evangelischen Theologie,* vol. 2 (4th ed.; Gütersloh: Gerd Mohn, 1968), p. 378.

4. Fr. D. E. Schleiermacher, *Hermeneutik,* ed. Heinz Kimmerle (Heidelberg: Carl Winter Universitätsverlag, 1959), p. 31.

5. Ludwig Wittgenstein, *Philosophical Investigations,* trans. G. E. M. Anscombe, ed. G. E. M. Anscombe and Rush Rhees (3d ed.; New York: Macmillan Co., 1958), p. 432.

6: Hermeneutics and the Authority of Scripture

1. David H. Kelsey, *The Uses of Scripture in Recent Theology* (Philadelphia: Fortress Press, 1975), p. 97. There are, of course, other definitions of "scripture," but this one best serves my purposes here. In most of the occurrences of "scripture" in this chapter, the term "canon" might serve as well. For other purposes, the terms are not synonymous.

2. See, for example, Elisabeth Schüssler Fiorenza, *Bread Not Stone: The Challenge of Feminist Biblical Interpretation* (Boston: Beacon Press, 1984), pp. 9–11, 61. As Schüssler Fiorenza acknowledges (p. 161, n. 39), she borrows the contrast from Rachel Blau DuPlessis.

3. Ibid., pp. 13–14. Just how this alternative, extrabiblical canon is to be identified and understood is less clear from Schüssler Fiorenza's essays than is her critique of biblical authority. The question of whether this feminist canon is to be understood also as the Christian canon — and, if so, on what grounds — is especially intriguing.

4. Delwin Brown, "Struggle till Daybreak: On the Nature of Authority in Theology," *Journal of Religion* 65 (1985): 15–32, esp. 20–26. Brown's "authoring model" trades on the sense of *exousia*, which is closer to "power" than to "authority" when these terms are distinguished. The model has so little to do with the latter concept that his attempt to offer it as a redefinition of biblical and theological authority faces some significant difficulties. Whether an alternative approach is able to escape his strictures against the "authorization model" is another question.

5. See, for example, Schubert M. Ogden, "What Is Theology?" *Journal of Religion* 52 (1972): 22–40; and Kelsey, *Uses of Scripture,* pp. 153–54. Ogden has since refined his account of theological inquiry, with reference to Jürgen Habermas's analysis of the "validity claims" made or implied in discourse and action; see, for example, Schubert M. Ogden, "The Service of Theology to the Servant Task of Pastoral Ministry," in *The Pastor as Servant,* ed. Earl E. Shelp and Ronald H. Sunderland (New York: Pilgrim Press, 1986), pp. 87–93. For yet another account of the sorts of questions involved in theological inquiry, see Charles M. Wood, *Vision and Discernment: An Orientation in Theological Study* (Atlanta: Scholars Press, 1985), ch. 3.

6. Kelsey, *Uses of Scripture,* ch. 8.

7. Harry Y. Gamble, *The New Testament Canon: Its Making and Meaning* (Philadelphia: Fortress Press, 1985), p. 75.

8. Ibid. The whole of Gamble's work, and especially the last chapter, is instructive on our topic. See also Brevard S. Childs, *The New Testament as Canon: An Introduction* (Philadelphia: Fortress Press, 1984), ch. 4.

9. George A. Lindbeck, *The Nature of Doctrine: Religion and Theology in a Postliberal Age* (Philadelphia: Westminster Press, 1984), pp. 113–24.

10. Hans W. Frei, "The 'Literal Reading' of Biblical Narrative in the Christian Tradition: Does It Stretch or Will It Break?" in *The Bible and the Narrative Tradition,* ed. Frank McConnell (New York: Oxford University Press, 1986), p. 72. Frei goes on to argue that "the literal sense is the paradigmatic form of such intratextual interpretation in the Christian community's use of its scripture."

11. Lindbeck, *Nature of Doctrine,* p. 114. Cited in Frei, " 'Literal Reading' of Biblical Narrative," p. 72.

12. E. D. Watt, in one of the more discriminating and helpful of recent treatments of the concept of authority, writes: "Authority is never egalitarian. An authority is always a superior of some kind, to be obeyed in some cases, in other cases to be followed, consulted, attended to, deferred to, or conformed to.... Authority in all its forms is associated with, and is a constant reminder of, some human limitation, weakness, or dependency" (*Authority* [New York: St. Martin's Press, 1982], p. 7).

7: On Being Known

1. Otto Michel, *Der Brief an die Hebräer* (12th ed.; Göttingen: Vandenhoeck & Ruprecht, 1966), p. 197.

2. Martin Luther, "Lectures on Hebrews," trans. Walter A. Hanson, in *Luther's Works*, vol. 29, ed. Jaroslav Pelikan (St. Louis: Concordia Publishing House, 1968), p. 165.

3. Ibid., p. 167.

4. Martin Luther, "Lectures on Galatians (1535)," in *Luther's Works*, vol. 26, trans. and ed. Jaroslav Pelikan (St. Louis: Concordia Publishing House, 1963), p. 401.

5. Benjamin Jowett, "On the Interpretation of Scripture," in *Essays and Reviews* (6th ed.; London: Longman, Green, Longman, and Roberts, 1861), pp. 333-34.

6. The aptness of that designation is questionable, as, for example, Willi Marxsen indicates in the case of Luther in a recent essay, "Historisch-kritische Exegese?" in *Kirchlicher Dienst und theologische Ausbildung*, ed. Helmut Begeman and Carl Heinz Ratschow (Bielefeld: Luther Verlag, 1985), pp. 53-62.

8: On the Reality of God

1. Kai Nielsen, "Wisdom and Dilman on the Reality of God," *Religious Studies* 16 (1980): 54. His "principal target" is Ilham Dilman, "Wisdom's Philosophy of Religion," *Canadian Journal of Philosophy* 5 (1975): 473-521. For Nielsen's understanding of "Wittgensteinian fideism," see his article by that title in *Philosophy* 42 (1967): 191-209. The term does not appear in the more recent article.

2. Nielsen, "Wisdom and Dilman on the Reality of God," p. 60.

3. John Wisdom, "Gods," in *Philosophy and Psycho-analysis* (Oxford: Basil Blackwell, 1965), p. 154.

4. Dilman, "Wisdom's Philosophy of Religion," pp. 474-76.

5. Ibid., p. 519.

6. Ludwig Wittgenstein, *Philosophical Investigations*, trans. G. E. M. Anscombe, ed. G. E. M. Anscombe and Rush Rhees (3d ed.; New York: Macmillan Co., 1958), sec. 373.

7. Alfred North Whitehead, *Religion in the Making* (Cleveland: World Publishing Co., 1960), p. 82.

9: The Events in Which God Acts

1. Friedrich Schleiermacher, *On Religion: Speeches to Its Cultured Despisers*, trans. John Oman (New York: Harper & Row, 1958), p. 88.

2. Friedrich Schleiermacher, *The Christian Faith*, vol. 1, ed. H. R. Mackintosh and J. S. Stewart (New York: Harper & Row, 1963), p. 215. See Robert R. Williams, *Schleiermacher the Theologian: The Construction of the Doctrine of God* (Philadelphia: Fortress Press, 1978), pp. 90–95.

3. Martin Luther, "Against the Heavenly Prophets in the Matter of Images and Sacraments (1525)," in *Luther's Works*, vol. 40, trans. and ed. Conrad Bergendoff (Philadelphia: Muhlenberg Press, 1958), pp. 212–13.

4. Cited in Horst Georg Pöhlmann, *Abriss der Dogmatik* (2d ed.; Gütersloh: Gerd Mohn, 1975), p. 232.

10: The Aim of Christian Theology

1. The citation, found in section 13 of Wesley's preface, corresponds to a citation in section 14 of the Praefatio of J. A. Bengel's *Gnomon Novi Testamenti*, to which Wesley was heavily indebted: "Lutherus ait, Nil aliud esse Theologiam, atque Grammaticam, in Spiritus sancti verbis occupatam." I have not been able to locate the remark itself in Luther.

2. Ludwig Wittgenstein, *Philosophical Investigations*, trans. G. E. M. Anscombe, ed. G. E. M. Anscombe and Rush Rhees (3d. ed.; New York: Macmillan Co., 1958), sec. 373.

3. Quoted in Gottfried Hornig, *Die Anfänge der historisch-kritischen Theologie* (Göttingen: Vandenhoeck & Ruprecht, 1961), p. 69.

4. Karl Barth, *Church Dogmatics* I/1, trans. G. W. Bromiley (Edinburgh: T. & T. Clark, 1975), p. 113.

5. Ernst Käsemann, "The Canon of the New Testament and the Unity of the Church," in *Essays on New Testament Themes* (London: SCM Press, 1964), pp. 222–23.

6. G. E. Moore, "Wittgenstein's Lectures in 1930–33," in *Philosophical Papers* (New York: Collier, 1962), p. 271.

7. Wittgenstein, *Philosophical Investigations*, sec. 373; cf. sec. 29.

8. Ludwig Wittgenstein, *Zettel*, trans. G. E. M. Anscombe (Oxford: Basil Blackwell, 1967), sec. 144.

9. Quoted in Gerhard Ebeling, *Introduction to a Theological Theory of Language*, trans. R. A. Wilson (London: Collins, 1973), pp. 134–35.

10. Wittgenstein, *Philosophical Investigations*, sec. 497.

Index

Allen, Joseph L., 110 n.5
apprehension, 42–44
aptitude, 4–5
Augustine, 97
Austin, J. L., 73, 78
authority
  de facto, 61
  de jure, 62
  and narrative, 65
  three questions of, 61–62

Barth, Karl, 8, 35, 100, 101
Bengel, J. A., 115, n.1
Boehler, Peter, 37
Brown, Delwin, 59, 64–65
Bultmann, Rudolf, 110 n.6
Burrell, David, 11

Calvin, John, 35, 37
canon, 67–68, 102–3
Christian, William A., 110 n.4
Christian education, 13–14
Cone, James, 111 n.2
Congar, Yves, 101
conventions, 49–50, 52, 66

Dilman, Ilham, 83–87

Edwards, Jonathan, 43
experience, 38–42

Fiorenza, Elisabeth Schüssler,
  58–59, 64

Foster, George Burman, 8
Foster, Michael, 111 n.8
Frei, Hans, 46, 65, 68, 113 n.10

Gamble, Harry Y., 67
grammar, 86–87, 103
  theology as, 98–108

imagination, 40–42
intertextuality, 67–68
intratextuality, 68–70

Jowett, Benjamin, 75–76
judgment, 5, 18

Kant, Immanuel, 36–37
Käsemann, Ernst, 100
Kelsey, David H., 30, 57, 62, 64,
  111 n.6

Lindbeck, George, 26–27, 68–69
Lonergan, Bernard, 43
Luther, Martin, 7, 39–40, 46, 72,
  75, 96, 98, 103

Míguez Bonino, José, 111 n.2
ministry, 11–13

Nielsen, Kai, 83–87

Oden, Thomas C., 110 n.8
Ogden, Schubert M., 62, 110 n.6

Pascal, Blaise, 37, 41

sacraments, 96–97
Schleiermacher, Friedrich, 48, 90
Semler, Johann Salomo, 99, 107

theological education, 3–4, 15–16,
    28, 29–30, 32
theology
  Christian, 4–5
  historical, 22
  pastoral, 22–23
  philosophical, 22
  practical, 21–23
Tillich, Paul, 81

validity, 15
vocation
  Christian, 12
  human, 11–12

Walzer, Michael, 29
Watt, E. D., 113 n.12
Wesley, John, 37, 43, 98
Whitehead, A. N., 87
Wilkes, Paul, 110 n.1
Wisdom, John, 83–85
Wittgenstein, Ludwig, 38, 41,
    42, 49, 86, 88, 98, 103,
    106
Wolff, Christian, 46–48